Collins

Enhanced

Science Now

A Science Textbook based on Holistic Learning Theory

4

Name : ....

Grade : .... Section : ....

I'm a carnivorous plant and I've got an amazing skill! I can actually count! When something gently touches my special hairs, I remain composed and keep my trap open. However, if it touches me multiple times quickly, I snap shut, knowing it's time for dinner! I'm a clever plant, conserving energy by capturing real food. What am I? ....

Series Editor | Jyothsna Natraj

HarperCollins*Publishers*

Publishing operations in 17 countries and 120+ imprints globally

William Collins' dream of knowledge for all began with the publication of his first book in 1819. A self-educated mill worker, he not only enriched millions of lives, but also founded a flourishing publishing house. Today, staying true to this spirit, Collins books are packed with inspiration, innovation and practical expertise. They place you at the centre of a world of possibility and give you exactly what you need to explore it.

Published by Collins Learning
An imprint of HarperCollins*Publishers* India
Building No. 10, Tower A, 4th Floor, DLF Cyber City, Gurugram, Haryana 122002, India

First edition: 2024
Reprint edition: 2025
ISBN: 978-93-6213-956-6

Content developed by **Excelsoft Technologies Pvt Ltd.**
Artwork, typesetting and layout by **AptaraCorp Ltd., Mammoth Studioz Ltd, iBook Services**
Printed and bound in India by Saurabh Printers Pvt. Ltd.

ACKNOWLEDGEMENTS

Title Page: Alfsky

Inside: Page **4:** Tomas Knopp; **18:** pixel107; **20:** CoolKengzz, Olympus; **21:** Super Prin, Kokhanchikov, Grigorev Mikhail, Ksenica, bauhaus1000; **22:** Ruud Morijn Photographer, roundstripe, Nelson Sirlin; **23:** Nithid Memanee, asif waseem; **24:** themorningglory, wichitpong katwit, Pakhnyushcha; a9photo; **25:** Decha Thapanya, dabjola, Julia Pivovarova; **29:** Decha Thapanya, Kokhanchikov, Nelson Sirlin; **30:** KanKhem; **41:** LokFung, Volodymyr Kryshtal; **43:** outdoorsman, Daniel Prudek, Gillian Holliday; **44:** Xavier MARCHANT, worldswildlifewonders; **45:** MNSKumar, rickyd; **46:** Wanchai Orsuk; **47:** Ratchapol Yindeesuk, Stephane Bidouze; **48:** Cathy Keifer, neelsky; **52:** Gillian Holliday, Daniel Prudek, Xavier MARCHANT, outdoorsman, Cathy Keifer, MNSKumar, Stephane Bidouze, Ratchapol Yindeesuk; **54:** James Warwick, Tristan Brown, Arthur Machado, Photo by K S Kong; **63:** Peter Dazeley; **64:** Multiart, glasscuter, v.s.anandhakrishna, highviews, Anna Breitenberger, windu, mygoodpix, Elena Larina; **65:** Evgenia Sh., Hurst Photo; **66:** Robyn Mackenzie, zkruger, Kondor83, Hong Vo, Dancestrokes, Tischenko Irina, Evgeny Karandaev, Elena Schweitzer, ALEAIMAGE; **67:** elenabs; **68:** Ljupco Smokovski, Laborant, grynold, Madlen, monticello; **73:** Kondor83, Robyn Mackenzie, Elena Schweitzer, Tischenko Irina, Evgeny Karandaev, Dancestrokes, ALEAIMAGE, Hurst Photo; **74:** Gurzzza; Ed Reschke; **86:** VasjaKoman, yukipon, jattumongkhon, newannyart; **88:** CasPRO; **90:** Bombaert Patrick, 3Dstock; **95:** habun; **100:** Carlos Caetano; **108:** zaricm, colematt; **109:** MaxPhoto, Santia; **114:** ttsz; **118:** ttsz; **120:** anuwat meereewee; **127:** kbeis; **129:** bjul; **130:** Linda Holt Ayriss; **134:** Linda Holt Ayriss; **138:** Aluna1; **148:** colematt; **149:** Dmytro Bochkov; **151:** Vect0r0vich; **155:** Pavel Ganchev- Paf, ssuaphotos, Colin Stitt; **159:** 5ociq, nito, Moon Light PhotoStudio; **160:** blueringmedia, jamesjoong, anuwat meereewee, ilyast

Supplementary Booklet: Icon_Craft_Studio, Olesia Kononenko, Julia_Sudnitskaya, Dynamic Graphics, andegro4ka, Poppy Hollis, fahima sultana chowdhury, AlionaManakova, Lesia_G, Good_Stock, AlionaManakova, sarunyu_foto, eliflamra

Browse the complete Collins catalogue at www.collins.in.
For any queries/feedback, please write to us at SCHOOLSUPPORT@harpercollins.co.in.

Preface

We live in a rapidly changing world where a person's decision can have an impact on the environment and others. Should the learning approach remain the same? What type of learning and skills should be developed so that students can face the demands and challenges of everyday life and succeed in the 21st century? One way of achieving this would be adopting the *holistic learning theory*.

Holistic learning theory or *holistic education* implies that each person finds identity, meaning and purpose in life through connections to the community, to the natural world and to values such as compassion and peace. It strives to help learners grow in all dimensions: intellectual, emotional, social, artistic, moral, psychological, physical, aesthetic, creative, intuitive and spiritual.

Enhanced Science Now, a series of eight books for Classes 1 to 8, adheres to the guidelines of the *National Education Policy* (NEP) 2020 and adopts the *holistic learning theory*. This enhanced edition retains the focus of the original edition, where the development of lateral thinking, analytical, research and deduction skills in students were encouraged. While the strong content would help strengthen the knowledge of the core science subject, new features based on the holistic learning theory would help in the development of every student's intellectual, emotional, social, artistic and creative potentials. This enhanced edition, thus, is an attempt to provide meaningful learning and help the students become well-rounded adults, ready to face the challenges in the 21st century, and ultimately empower the students to discover their full potential as learners.

Key Features

- **Summary** Snapshot of the chapter in the form of a graphic organizer for quick revision
- **Exercise** Questions dealing with Remembering and Understanding levels of Bloom's taxonomy
- **Cognitive Corner** Section dealing with Applying, Analysing, Evaluating and Creating levels of Bloom's taxonomy and Life Skills
- **Worksheets** Pictorial exercises based on the United Nations Sustainable Development Goals
- **Skills You Need** A variety of interesting information and activities to introduce skill courses with some form of experiential learning
- **Happiness Activity Sheets** A variety of interesting activities based on life skills, self-awareness, other awareness, emotional needs and mental needs
- **Vernacular Names** List of plants and animals used in the book and their names in a few Indian regional languages
- **STEAM Activities** Engaging STEAM-based activities for the future problem solvers, critical thinkers, innovators and inventors

Four **assessment papers** and two **comprehensive assessment papers** have been given, in addition to the exercises at the end of each chapter.

The **Series Editor** for classes 1 to 5 is **Jyothsna Natraj**, a teacher at Vidya Mandir Senior Secondary School. She has been teaching science for over a decade. She has experience in web-based content development and has extensively used technologies such as 'SMART' tools in her classes.

Feedback, valuable comments and suggestions from the users are welcome.

Authors

Key Features

The key features of ***Enhanced Science Now*** are completely aligned with the **National Education Policy** (NEP) 2020, and have been designed based on the *holistic learning theory* to facilitate a holistic education. These features not only aim at the development of intellectual capabilities of the students but also aim at the development of physical capabilities, intellectual abilities, cognitive or mental abilities, emotional abilities and social skills.

Multifaceted features such as Cognitive Corner, Life Skills, Worksheet, Skills You Need, Happiness Activity Sheets and STEAM Activities would help in the holistic development of a student through interesting questions, projects and activities while providing experiential learning and fostering innovative thinking and creativity.

The series also aims at making the students aware of the **Sustainable Developments Goals (SDGs)**. The SDGs are the 17 Global Goals adopted by all United Nations Member States in 2015 to help end poverty, protect the planet and ensure peace and prosperity for all by 2030. Read more about the goals at https://www.un.org/sustainabledevelopment/

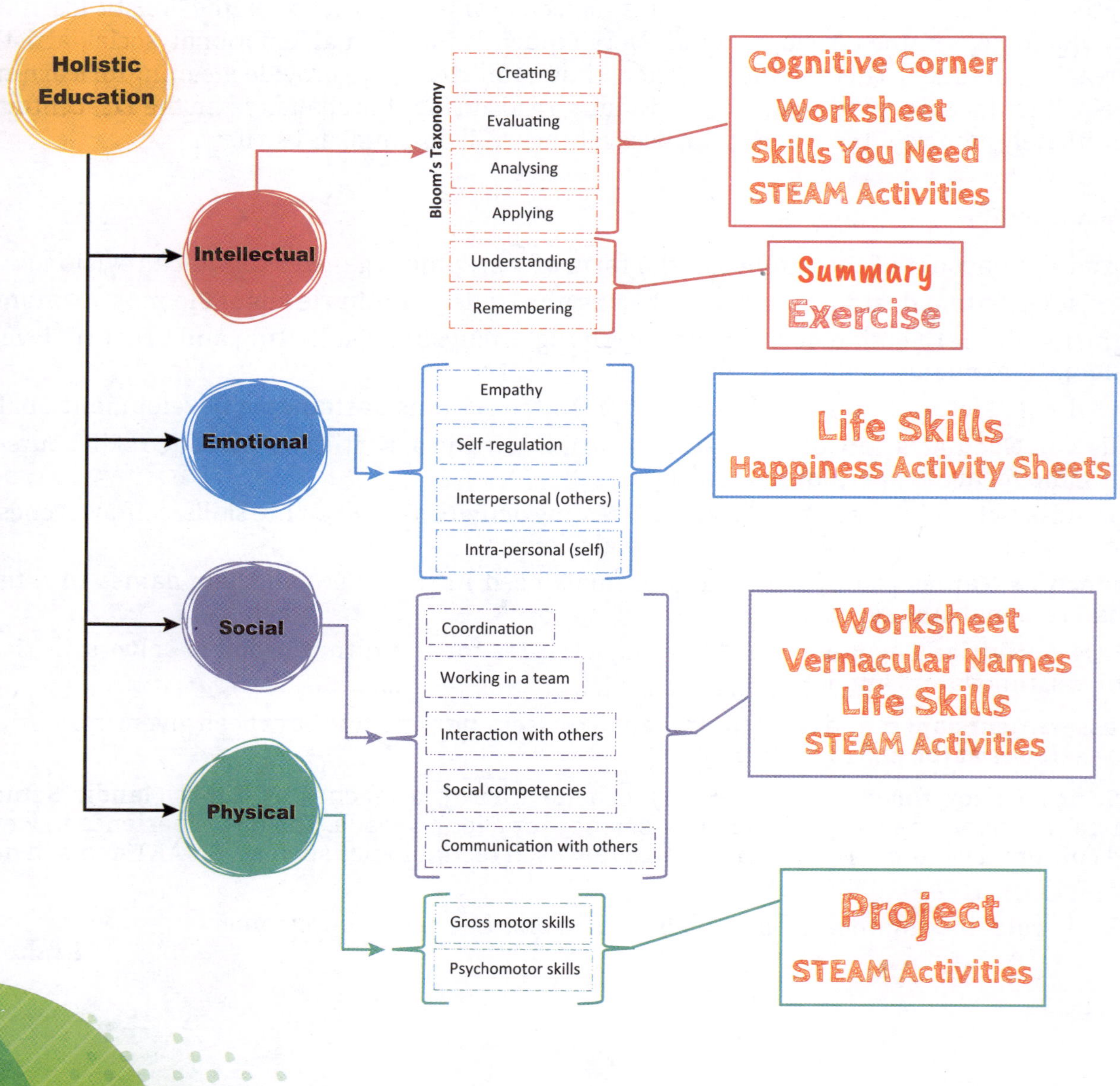

About the Features

Summary

Snapshot of the chapter in the form of a graphic organizer for quick revision

Exercise

Questions dealing with Remembering and Understanding levels of Bloom's taxonomy

Cognitive Corner

Section dealing with Applying, Analysing, Evaluating and Creating levels of Bloom's taxonomy

Critical Thinking Questions to address cognitive development such as thinking, reasoning, analysis, inference and drawing conclusions

Picture Study Questions to help develop observation and inference skills

Project Ideas for experiential learning and subject enrichment with cross-curricular links

Life Skills

Thought-provoking passage and relevant questions to help develop sensible life skills such as self-awareness, empathy and attitude towards self and others

Worksheet

Pictorial exercises at the end of each chapter based on the United Nations Sustainable Development Goals

Collins Learning supports the Sustainable Development Goals

Skills You Need

A variety of interesting information and activities to introduce skill courses with some form of experiential learning

Happiness Activity Sheets

A variety of interesting activities based on life skills, self-awareness, other awareness, emotional needs and mental needs

Vernacular Names

List of plants and animals used in the book and their names in a few Indian regional languages

STEAM Activities

Engaging STEAM-based activities for the future problem solvers, critical thinkers, innovators and inventors

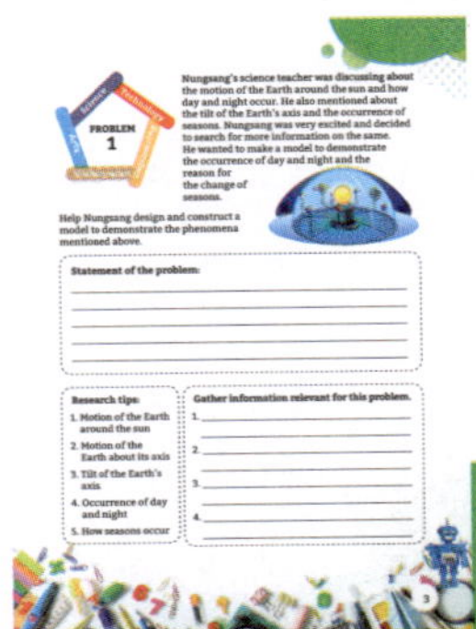

Contents

Unit 1 Plant World

1. The Green Plants 7
2. Plant Adaptations 19

Unit 2 Animal World

3. Animals and Their Young Ones 31
4. Animal Adaptations 42

Unit 3 Human Body and Health

5. Circulatory System and Excretory System 55
6. Food: Our Basic Need 64
7. Digestion of Food 75
8. Clothes 87

Unit 4 Nature, Environment and Space

9. Air, Water and Weather 96
10. The Solar System 109
11. Keeping the Earth Green 121

Unit 5 Materials and Matter

12. Soil 128
13. Solids, Liquids and Gases 139
14. Force, Work and Energy 150

1 The Green Plants

Learning Checklist

- Leaf
- How do plants make their food?
- Interdependence of plants and animals

Let's Get Started

Leaves of different plants differ in shape, size and colour. Look at the pictures of leaves given below and fill in the blanks using the given words.

long needle-like coloured

The leaves are ____________

The leaves are ____________

The leaf is ____________

Let us learn more about leaves and their functions in this chapter.

LEAF

a

A leaf is a flat structure growing from the stem or branch of a plant. Most plants have green leaves. The green colour is due to the presence of a pigment[1] called **chlorophyll** in the leaves.

The flat part of the leaf is called the **leaf blade** or **lamina**. The part that attaches the leaf to the stem or branch, or supports the leaf is called the ***petiole***. Leaf has a main vein called the **midrib** and many small veins branching off from it. These small veins transport water, minerals and nutrients to and from the leaves of a plant.

> **Word Web**
>
> [1]**Pigment**: coloured substance

The underside of every leaf has tiny openings called **stomata** (*singular*: stoma). Stomata help the plants to breathe. Two bean-shaped structures called **guard cells** surround the stomata. Guard cells control the opening and closing of stomata.

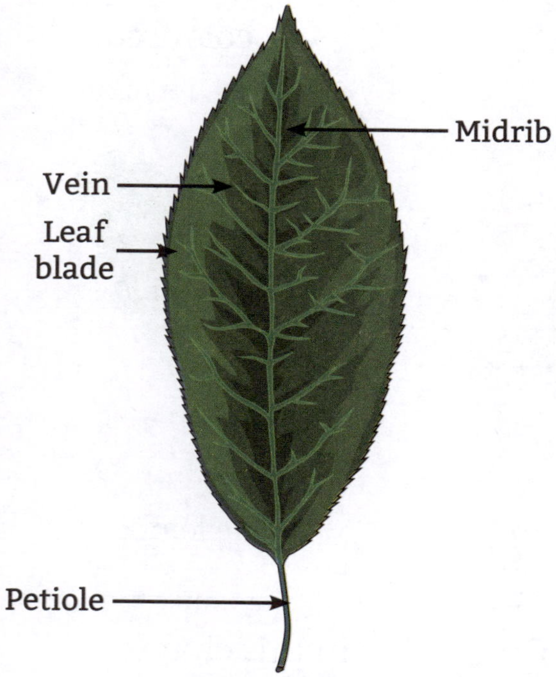

Parts of a leaf

Leaf cells

HOW DO PLANTS MAKE THEIR FOOD?

a

Green plants make their own food by a process called **photosynthesis** (*photo* means light and *synthesis* means to put together). Photosynthesis takes place in the leaves; that is why leaves are called the food factory or the kitchen of a plant.

The following things are required by a plant to carry out photosynthesis:

- Carbon dioxide
- Light
- Water
- Chlorophyll

Light is mostly obtained from the sun. Chlorophyll present in the green leaves absorbs the sunlight. Carbon dioxide enters the leaves through stomata. Water is taken in by the roots and carried to the leaves by the stem. The products of photosynthesis are sugar and oxygen.

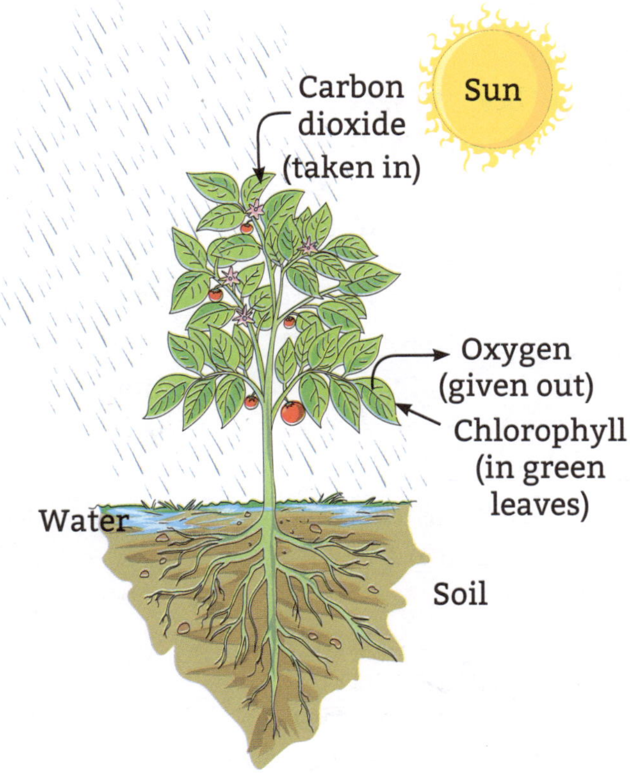

Photosynthesis

$$\text{Carbon dioxide} + \text{Water} \xrightarrow[\text{Chlorophyll}]{\text{Light}} \text{Sugar} + \text{Oxygen}$$

Plants use the prepared food for growth and other functions. Extra food is stored in the form of starch in different parts of a plant.

Activity 1

Aim: To show that leaves prepare food which is stored in the form of starch

Materials required: A potted plant, black paper, beaker, burner, water, forceps, Petri-plate, dropper, alcohol and iodine solution

Note: To be performed as a teacher demonstration

Procedure:

1. Keep the potted plant in a dark room for two or three days.
2. Clip some black paper to a green leaf of the plant. Keep the plant exposed to sunlight for one day.
3. Remove the black paper from the leaf.
4. Take some water in a small beaker and heat it on a burner.
5. Dip the leaf into the boiling water with the help of forceps. Keep it for about two minutes.
6. Remove the leaf from the boiling water and dip it completely in alcohol.
7. Heat the set-up using a burner until the leaf turns white.
8. Take out the leaf carefully using forceps and wash it with cold water.
9. Place it on the Petri-plate and pour a few drops of iodine solution over it with the help of a dropper.

Black paper clamped to a leaf

Leaf boiled in water

Leaf dipped in alcohol

Adding iodine solution

Colour change in leaf

Observation: The portion of the leaf that was exposed to sunlight turns to blue-black in colour, while the portion covered with the black paper does not change colour.

Conclusion: The blue-black colour indicates the presence of starch and is a positive result for starch test. The portion of the leaf that was exposed to sunlight was able to prepare its food and store starch. The portion covered with the black paper could not prepare its food because it did not receive any sunlight. Thus, no starch formation took place in this part of the leaf.

Revise and Recall

1. Look at the picture of a leaf shown below and fill in the names of its parts.

2. Select the words from the help box and fill in the blanks.

Oxygen, Light, Chlorophyll, Sugar, Carbon dioxide, Water

Photosynthesis is:

________ + ________ ⟶ ________ + ________

INTERDEPENDENCE OF PLANTS AND ANIMALS

Plants and animals depend on each other for their survival.

Plants produce their own food by the process of photosynthesis and give out oxygen in this process. The oxygen given out by plants is necessary for human beings and animals to survive. Animals also depend on plants for food.

> **Science in Context**
>
> Plants not only provide us with food to eat and oxygen to breathe, but also provide us with medicines. Many medicines that we use are made from plants.

Herbivorous animals eat plants as their food. Carnivores depend on the herbivores for their food. Plants are eaten by herbivores, which in turn are eaten by carnivores, thus forming a chain. A chain that shows how one organism is dependent on another organism for food is called a **food chain**.

Grass eaten by grasshopper → Grasshopper eaten by frog → Frog eaten by snake → Snake eaten by hawk →

A food chain

Animals help plants by carrying their seeds to far-off places for dispersal[1]. Animals breathe out carbon dioxide, which is used by plants for photosynthesis.

Interdependence of plants and animals

> **Word Web**
>
> [1]**Dispersal:** the action of spreading things over a wide area
>
> [2]**Interdependence**: dependence on each other

The interdependence[2] of plants and animals creates a balance in nature. If the number of either plants or animals increases or decreases suddenly, this balance will be disturbed.

If there is a sudden decrease in the number of plants in nature, the oxygen level in the atmosphere will decrease, leading to an increase in the level of carbon dioxide. Similarly, if there is a sudden increase in the number of animals in nature, it will lead to an outbreak of diseases and insufficient food to meet the needs of the growing population.

Revise and Recall

Match the following.

1. Animals give out	(a) chlorophyll
2. Green plants	(b) carbon dioxide
3. Plants give us	(c) interdependent
4. Plants and animals are	(d) seed dispersal
5. Animals help plants in	(e) food and oxygen

Keywords

Chlorophyll: The pigment that gives green colour to the leaves

Stomata: Tiny openings on the underside of leaves that help the plant to breathe

Petiole: The part of a leaf that holds it to the stem or the branch of the plant

Photosynthesis: The process by which plants make their own food, using water and carbon dioxide in the presence of light and chlorophyll

Food chain: The chain that shows how one organism is dependent on another organism for its food

Summary

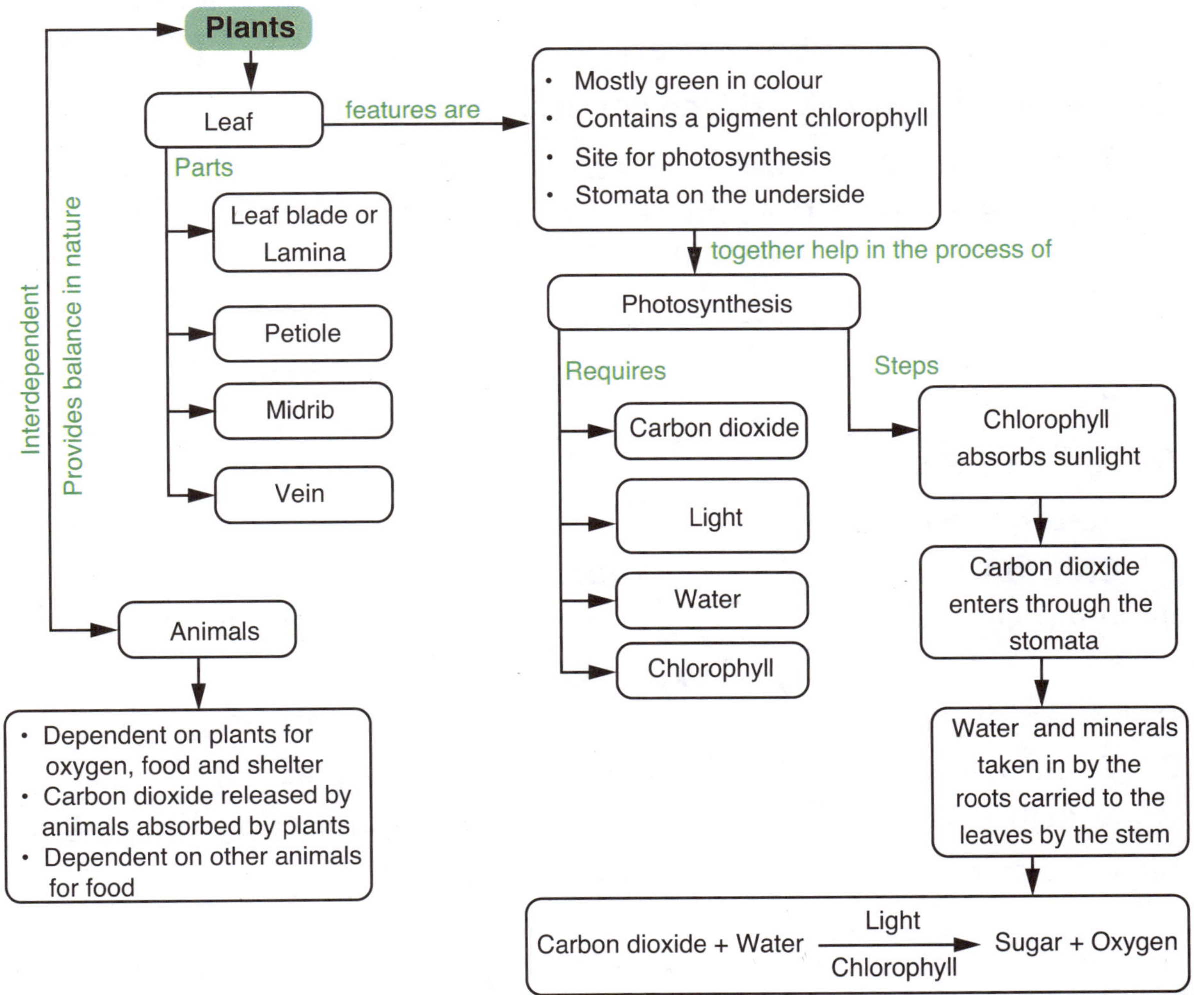

Exercise

W

A. Choose the correct option for each of the following. ia

1. Leaves are green in colour due to the presence of
   (a) Stomata (b) Chlorophyll (c) Carbon dioxide (d) Oxygen
2. The part of a leaf that attaches it to the stem or branch is called
   (a) Midrib (b) Blade (c) Petiole (d) Vein
3. Plants make their own food using
   (a) Carbon dioxide (b) Sunlight
   (c) Water (d) All of these
4. During photosynthesis, plants produce
   (a) Sunlight (b) Sugar
   (c) Carbon dioxide (d) All of these
5. Which of these substances do veins transport to and from leaves?
   (a) Water (b) Minerals (c) Nutrients (d) All of these

B. Fill in the blanks with the correct words. ia

1. The flat part of a leaf is called ________________. (vein/leaf blade)
2. Tiny openings on the underside of leaves of plants are called ________________. (stomata/vein)
3. Chlorophyll gives ________________ colour to the plant. (white/green)
4. Plants give us ________________ to breathe. (oxygen/carbon dioxide)
5. Animals breathe out ________________. (carbon dioxide/oxygen)

C. Match the following.

Column A	**Column B**
1. Photosynthesis	(a) Attaches the leaf to the stem or branch
2. Chlorophyll	(b) Transport substances
3. Veins	(c) Main vein of a leaf
4. Midrib	(d) Preparation of food by the plants
5. Petiole	(e) Green pigment

D. State whether the following statements are true (T) or false (F).

1. The midrib branches into smaller structures called veins. ☐
2. Leaves need light to make food. ☐
3. Leaves give out oxygen through the veins. ☐
4. Iodine changes the colour of a leaf containing starch to red. ☐
5. Animals do not depend on plants for food. ☐
6. In a food chain, one organism is the food for another organism. ☐

E. Name the following.

1. Bean-shaped structure that surrounds the stomata ____________
2. The pigment that helps plants in absorbing sunlight ____________
3. The form in which extra food is stored in plant parts ____________
4. A gas which is the product of photosynthesis ____________

F. Give reasons for the following.

1. Animals depend not only on plants, but also on other animals.
2. Water is transported from roots to leaves of a green plant.
3. The number of plants and animals must be balanced in nature.
4. Plants cannot make food without chlorophyll.
5. A bleached leaf turns blue-black in colour when iodine is added.

G. Answer the following questions briefly.

1. What is the function of veins in a leaf?
2. How do stomata help a leaf?
3. What is photosynthesis?
4. Explain the function of guard cells.
5. What is a food chain? Give your own example of a food chain.

H. Answer the following questions.

1. Explain the parts of a leaf with the help of a labelled diagram.
2. Name the four things that plants use to make food. From where do plants get these things?
3. Why is the interdependence of plants and animals important?

Cognitive Corner

Critical Thinking

1. Why is the upper part of all green leaves darker in colour than the underside of the leaves?
2. What would happen if you take a potted plant and lock it up inside a dark room for one week?

Picture Study

Complete the photosynthesis chart.

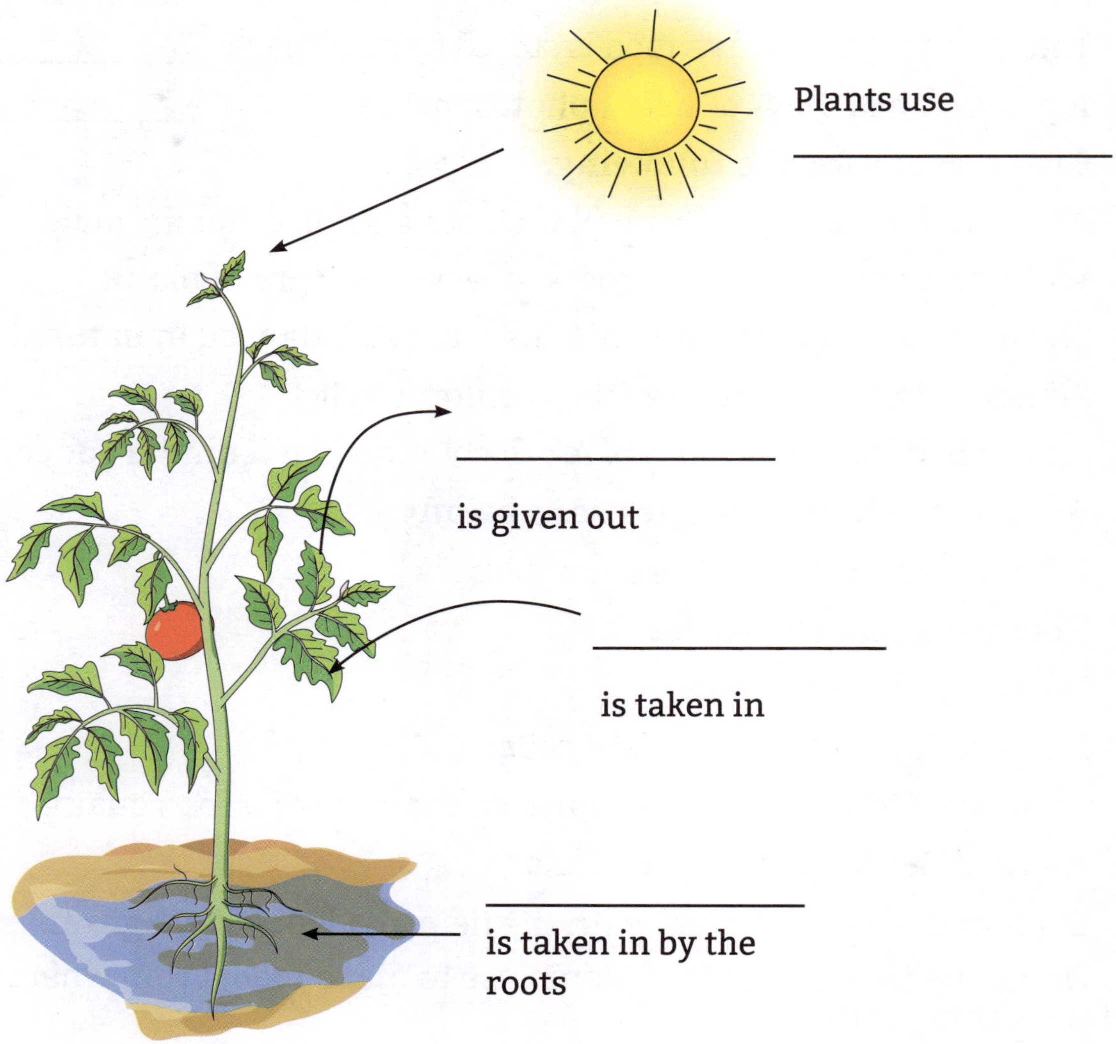

Project

Visit a greenhouse or a nursery in your village, city or town. Talk to the gardener, and find out the names of any five plants grown there and their uses. Prepare a report on your findings. If possible, include pictures of those plants.

Life Skills

Read the story of a tree and a woodcutter.

Plants are an important part of our lives. We get food to eat, fibres to make *clothes* and materials to build our houses from plants. We also get *medicines* from plants. Trees contribute to our environment by providing *oxygen*, *preserving soil* and *supporting wildlife*.

Now based on the story, write any five uses of trees.

1. ____________________
2. ____________________
3. ____________________
4. ____________________
5. ____________________

Why should we have more plants in our homes? What is the benefit of planting more trees?

Worksheet

Plants and animals are interdependent on each other. This interdependence creates a balance in nature. If this balance is disturbed, all the living organisms on this planet will suffer, in one way or another. The summer months are getting hotter, the winter months are lasting just a few months, the rainy days are not coming soon enough or not ending at some places, leading to flood; all these changes may be due to the disturbance in the balance in nature that we have created.

One small action you do can affect this balance, in a negative or a positive way.

A. What can you do so that you do not contribute to creating an imbalance in nature? Write down any three points.

B. How can you spread awareness among your family and friends about this topic? Draw a poster on the same and write a catchy slogan too.

2 Plant Adaptations

Learning Checklist

- Plant adaptations—aquatic, terrestrial, insectivorous, non-green, parasitic

Let's Get Started

Plants can be seen growing at all places. Look at the following pictures and use the words given in the box to fill in the blanks.

gardens	ponds	deserts	forests

Wild plants are found in ______________

Cacti are found in ______________

Lotus plants are found in ______________

Ornamental plants are found in ______________

The place where an organism naturally lives is called its **habitat**. The special features acquired by an organism to adjust itself in a habitat are called **adaptations**.

In this chapter, we will learn about different adaptations shown by plants.

PLANT ADAPTATIONS

Different kinds of plants grow in different places.

These plants adapt certain features to survive in their habitat. According to the habitat they grow in, plants can be broadly grouped into two categories: aquatic plants and terrestrial plants.

Aquatic Plants

a

Plants that grow and live in water are called **aquatic plants**. The following figure shows the different types of aquatic plants.

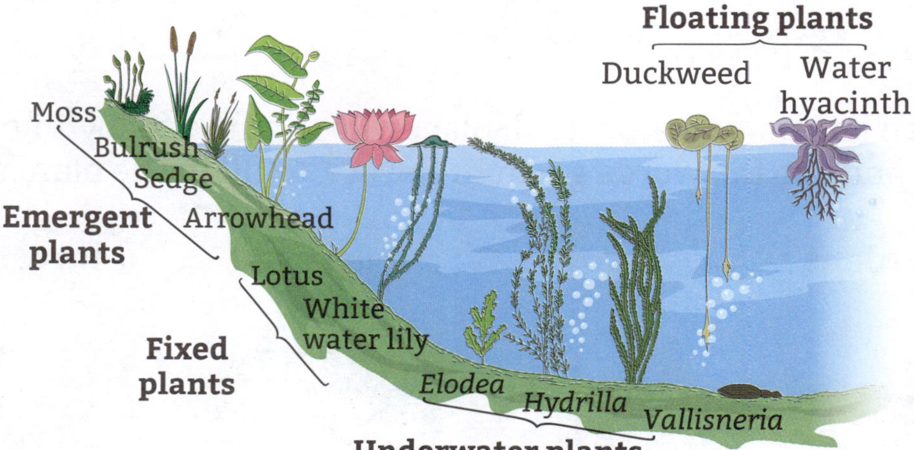

Emergent Plants

These plants are fixed to the shallow waterbed but their leaves and stems extend out of the surface of the water body they are growing in. Hence, these plants are called emergent plants. Examples of emergent plants are bulrush, cattail, arrowhead and sedge.

Bulrush

Sedge

The following adaptations are seen in these plants:

- These plants are usually tall.
- These plants usually have long, narrow leaves. Long and narrow leaves provide less resistance to strong water currents and wind, and hence, prevent damage.
- The stem of these plants are usually tough and hollow. Due to this, the plants do not get destroyed even in strong winds.

Fixed Plants

These plants are fixed to the waterbed with the help of strong roots. Hence, they are called fixed plants. Examples are lotus and water lily.

Lotus

Water lily

The following adaptations are seen in these plants:

- These plants have thin long stalks[1] that coil and uncoil according to the level of the water.
- Leaves are broad and have waxy coating to prevent them from getting wet.
- These plants have stomata on the upper side of the leaf.
- These plants absorb nutrients from the soil through their roots.

Word Web

[1]**Stalk**: a thin stem that supports the leaves and flowers of a plant

Underwater Plants

These plants grow completely under the water. Hence, they are also called submerged plants. Examples are *Hydrilla, Vallisneria* and pondweed.

The following adaptations are seen in these plants:

- These plants have thin, narrow, ribbon-like leaves to prevent them from getting torn by the force of water currents.
- The leaves of underwater plants do not have stomata but they take in carbon dioxide from the water through their body surface.
- These plants do not bear flowers.
- These plants get nutrients through the roots from the soil in the waterbeds.
- These plants support animal life to a great extent because they give out oxygen during photosynthesis, which keeps the aquatic animals alive.

Hydrilla

Vallisneria

Pondweed

Floating Plants

Duckweed

Water lettuce

Plants that float on water are called **floating plants**. Examples are duckweed, water lettuce and water hyacinth.

The following adaptations are seen in these plants:

- These plants float on water because either they have air filled inside their stems, for example, water hyacinth; or they are very small and light in weight, for example, duckweed.
- The roots of the floating plants hang in water and absorb nutrients directly from the water.

Revise and Recall

State whether the following statements are true (T) or false (F).

1. Water lettuce floats on water. ☐
2. Sedges are fixed in water and hence are called fixed plants. ☐
3. Fixed plants have stomata on the upper side of their leaves. ☐
4. Duckweed is an example of emergent plant. ☐
5. The arrowhead plants have leaves and stems emerging out of the water surface. ☐

Terrestrial Plants

a

Plants that grow on land are called **terrestrial plants**. Terrestrial plants grow in deserts, mountains and hills, plains, marshy areas, forests, coastal areas, etc.

Plants in Deserts

Desert plants are also called **xerophytes**. They are adapted to grow in very hot and dry conditions. Examples of plants that grow in deserts are date palms and *cacti* such as prickly pear.

A cactus growing in a desert

The following adaptations are seen in plants growing in a desert:

- The stem of a cactus is green, thick and fleshy. This helps the plant to collect and store water. It performs the function of photosynthesis.
- The leaves of these plants are modified to spines[1]. Spines protect the plants and reduce water loss.
- These plants also have long roots that grow deep into the ground. They help in absorbing groundwater.

Word Web

[1]**Spines**: sharp, pointed structures on a plant

Science in Context

Saguaro is a type of cactus found in deserts. It can live up to 200 years and can store up to 800 litres of water.

Plants on Mountains and Hills

Plants on mountains and hills are adapted to grow in very cold temperatures. Examples of such plants are pine, cedar, spruce and fir. The following adaptations are seen in these plants:

Pine tree

- The trees are straight, tall and cone-shaped so that snow can easily slide off their branches.
- Their leaves have a waxy coating and are needle-shaped, which helps the snow to slide off and prevents rotting of the plant.
- These plants have cones with seeds instead of flowers.

Plants in Plains

These plants are adapted to survive in varying climates of both hot and cold weather. Examples of plants that grow in plains are mango, banyan and teak. The following adaptations are seen in these plants:

Mango tree

- They have many branches with plenty of leaves and flowers.
- Some trees shed their leaves in autumn which grow back again during spring. Such trees are called **deciduous trees**.
- Some trees shed their leaves and grow new ones throughout the year. Such trees are called **evergreen trees**.

Plants in Marshy Areas

Mangroves

Marshy areas are places that have wet, clayey and sticky soil with water covering their surface. The plants growing in such areas develop roots that emerge out from the surface of the marsh. These roots help the plant to breathe. Hence, they are called **breathing roots**. Most of the plants that grow in marshy areas are called **mangroves**. Some examples are *Avicennia* and *Rhizophora*.

Plants in Forests

Forest

Forests usually have warm climates and get a lot of rain throughout the year. The plants that grow in forests grow tall with broad and abundant leaves, which can capture maximum sunlight for photosynthesis. Examples of plants that grow in forests are redwood, mahogany, maple and oak.

Plants in Coastal Areas

Coconut tree

Plants that grow in coastal areas usually grow tall and straight. They are adapted to survive in conditions of salty water and heavy rainfall. An example is a coconut tree.

Wonder!

There are about 600 types of carnivorous plants found all over the world, except in Antarctica.

Insectivorous Plants

Some plants live in a habitat where the soil is poor in nutrients. Some plants also grow in thick forests where enough sunlight is not available to carry out photosynthesis. These plants feed on small insects for nutrition. Hence, they are called **insectivorous plants**. Some examples are pitcher plant and venus flytrap.

Venus flytrap

Insectivorous plants show unique features that help them to catch their prey. The venus flytrap has two lobes with hair-like spikes on their edges. These lobes snap shut when an insect sits on it.

The pitcher plant is shaped like a pitcher. Its edges secrete a slippery substance due to which the insects sitting on it slip and fall inside the pitcher, thus getting trapped.

Pitcher plant

Non-green Plants

Some plants do not contain the green pigment chlorophyll and hence cannot carry out photosynthesis. Such plants are called **non-green plants**. These plants are adapted to absorb their food from dead plants and animals. Examples are coralroot and Indian pipe.

Indian pipe

Parasitic Plants

There are certain plants that depend on other plants partially or completely for their nutrition. They grow on other plants and absorb nutrients from the other plants. Such plants are called **parasitic plants**. They often harm the plant on which they grow. Examples are *Cuscuta* and mistletoe.

Cuscuta

Revise and Recall

Write an example for each of the following.

1. Desert plant __________
2. Mountain plant __________
3. Plant in plains __________
4. Plant in marshes __________
5. Insectivorous plant __________

Go Green

Walk through a park or a garden carefully. Tramping on small plants might kill them.

Keywords

Habitat: The place where an organism naturally lives

Adaptation: The special features acquired by an organism to adjust itself in a habitat

Aquatic plants: Plants that grow and live in water

Terrestrial plants: Plants that grow on land

Xerophytes: Plants that grow in deserts

Breathing roots: The roots developed by the plants growing in marshes, which emerge out from the surface of the marsh

Insectivorous plants: Plants that trap insects for obtaining nutrients

Parasitic plants: Plants that grow on other plants and absorb nutrients from them

Summary

Types of Plants

Based on habitat

- **Aquatic plants**
  - **Emergent plants** — *Adaptations*: Tall, long, narrow leaves, tough and hollow stem, both leaves and stem extend out of water. *Examples*: Bulrush and sedge
  - **Fixed plants** — *Adaptations*: Thin, long stalks, broad and waxy leaves, stomata on the upper side of the leaf, roots fixed to the soil. *Examples*: Lotus and water lily
  - **Underwater plants** — *Adaptations*: Thin, narrow, ribbon-like leaves, no stomata, do not bear flowers. *Examples*: *Hydrilla* and *Vallisneria*
  - **Floating plants** — *Adaptations*: Airy stems, lightweight. *Examples*: Water lettuce and duckweed
- **Terrestrial plants**
  - **Plants in deserts** — *Adaptations*: Thick and fleshy stem, leaves modified into spine, long roots. *Examples*: Cacti and date palms
  - **Plants in mountains and hills** — *Adaptations*: Straight, tall, cone-shaped trees, waxy leaves, cones with seeds instead of flowers. *Examples*: Pine and cedar
  - **Plants in plains** — *Adaptations*: Plenty of leaves and flowers, shedding of leaves in autumn or throughout the year and growth of new leaves. *Examples*: Mango and banyan
  - **Plants in marshy areas** — *Adaptations*: Breathing roots. *Examples*: *Avicennia* and *Rhizophora*
  - **Plants in forests** — *Adaptations*: Broad and abundant leaves. *Examples*: Redwood and oak
  - **Plants in coastal areas** — *Adaptations*: Tall and straight. *Example*: Coconut
- **Insectivorous plants** — *Adaptations*: Unique features to catch insects. *Example*: Lobes with hair-like spikes in Venus flytrap
- **Non-green plants** — *Adaptations*: Absence of chlorophyll, absorb food from dead plants and animals. *Example*: Indian pipe
- **Parasitic plants** — *Adaptations*: Grow on other plants and absorb food from these plants. *Example*: *Cuscuta*

Exercise

w

A. Choose the correct option for each of the following.

ia

1. Which of these plants floats on water?
   (a) Duckweed (b) Moss (c) Water lily (d) *Hydrilla*
2. Which of the following is a xerophyte?
   (a) Cactus (b) Teak (c) Pine (d) Maple
3. Plants that are adapted to grow in deserts have
   (a) Spines (b) Thin stem
   (c) Short roots (d) Many leaves
4. Terrestrial plants are found in
   (a) Deserts (b) Plains
   (c) Mountains (d) All these places
5. An example of a non-green plant is
   (a) Cedar (b) Coralroot
   (c) Venus flytrap (d) Oak

B. Fill in the blanks with the correct words.

ia

1. Arrowhead is an example of ________________ plant. (floating/emergent)
2. Mountain plants have ________________ leaves. (broad/needle-like)
3. Mangroves grow in ________________. (deserts/marshy areas)
4. ________________ traps and eats insects. (Cactus/Pitcher plant)
5. Non-green plants do not have ________________. (chlorophyll/stems)
6. *Cuscuta* is a ________________ plant. (parasitic/non-green)

C. Match the following.

	Column A		Column B
1.	Prickly pear	(a)	Mountain plant
2.	Pines	(b)	Plains
3.	Banyan	(c)	Insectivorous plant
4.	*Rhizophora*	(d)	Desert plant
5.	Venus flytrap	(e)	Mangroves

D. State whether the following statements are true (T) or false (F).

1. Water lily is a floating plant. ☐
2. Terrestrial plants can grow both on land and in water. ☐
3. Desert plants have thin stems. ☐
4. The leaves of deciduous trees are shed in autumn. ☐
5. Plants growing in coastal areas cannot survive in water. ☐

E. Name the following.

1. Plants having cones with seeds instead of flowers ____________
2. Plants that trap and eat insects ____________
3. Plants that remain completely submerged in water ____________
4. Plants that absorb food from dead plants and animals ____________
5. Plants that grow on other plants and often harm them ____________

F. Give reasons for the following.

1. Indian pipe plays an important role in maintaining the balance in nature.
2. Duckweed has air-filled stems.
3. *Avicennia* plant has breathing roots.
4. The edges of the pitcher of pitcher plant are slippery.
5. The leaves of plants in mountain region are needle-shaped and waxy.

G. Answer the following questions briefly.

1. What is adaptation?
2. Give two adaptations of underwater plants.
3. Give two examples each of emergent plants and parasitic plants.
4. Why do desert plants have thick stems?
5. Why does a lotus plant have a long stem?

H. Answer the following questions.

1. What are the different types of aquatic plants? Give one example for each.
2. List any two types of terrestrial plants and give one adaptation of each type.
3. How are parasitic plants different from insectivorous plants?
4. Discuss the adaptations of plants that grow in plains.
5. What are insectivorous plants? Explain with examples.

Cognitive Corner

Critical Thinking

1. A plant with broad leaves will not survive in a desert. Do you think this statement is correct? Explain.
2. What would happen to a mountain plant if the climate changes from very cold to hot and humid?

Picture Study

Write one main adaptation shown by these plants.

1. 

   ____

2. 

   ____

3. 

   ____

Project

1. Find out the different types of forests and the places where they are found. Refer to the books in your school library or use the Internet to get the information. Write the special features of plants that are adapted to grow in forests.
2. Write a letter to the forest authority telling them the benefits of plants and trees so that they do not allow cutting down of trees in the future.

Life Skills

We can take care of plants by taking small steps. We know that paper is made from plants. So, we should not waste paper and reuse it whenever possible. What steps do you take in your day-to-day life to take care of plants? List any three points.

Worksheet

Our Earth is an amazing place. On one hand, we have mountains that are never free of snow. On the other hand, we have deserts where it does not rain for days. Again, there are places where it rains every day.

Plants and animals living in these areas have learned to adapt to these conditions.

A. What types of plants grow in your neighbourhood? Identify any five plants.

____

____

____

____

B. By observing the plants, identify any two adaptations shown by the plants that allow the plant to survive in your neighbourhood.

____

____

____

____

C. Suppose there is a park in your neighbourhood. The park is a habitat to a variety of plants, and it is going to be destroyed to build a shopping mall. How would you feel? What can you do to save the park, and thus save the habitat of so many plants? Write down a few steps you would take to save the park.

____

____

____

____

____

____

3 Animals and Their Young Ones

Learning Checklist

- Animals that lay eggs
- Animals that give birth to babies

Let's Get Started

The eggs belong to one of these animals. Take the animal to its eggs by drawing a line.

Dog

Cat

Hen

Giraffe

Cow

Eggs

One of the characteristics of living beings is that they produce young ones of their own kind. This process is called **reproduction**.

Some animals lay eggs from which the young ones hatch, whereas other animals give birth to young ones directly without laying eggs. Let us learn more about how animals reproduce.

ANIMALS THAT LAY EGGS

Animals that reproduce by laying eggs are called **egg-laying animals**. Examples are birds, frogs, fish, snakes, lizards and insects such as cockroach and butterfly.

> **Science in Context**
>
> Egg-laying animals are also called oviparous animals.

The eggs are kept in a warm place or the parent animals sit on their eggs to keep them warm. This process is known as **incubation**.

Birds

Birds lay eggs in their nests and incubate the eggs by sitting on them until the eggs hatch into young ones. When the eggs hatch, chicks come out. They cannot fly as they are featherless and cannot see. The parent birds help them in feeding and take care of them until they develop feathers and learn to fly.

Hen sitting on eggs to incubate them

Chicks hatching from eggs

Hen and chicks

Structure of an egg

Eggs of all birds have the same kind of internal structure. The thin, hard outer layer that protects the contents of the egg is called the **egg shell**. The jelly-like white-coloured substance that is present inside the egg shell is called the **albumen**. The yellow-coloured substance present within the albumen is called the **yolk**.

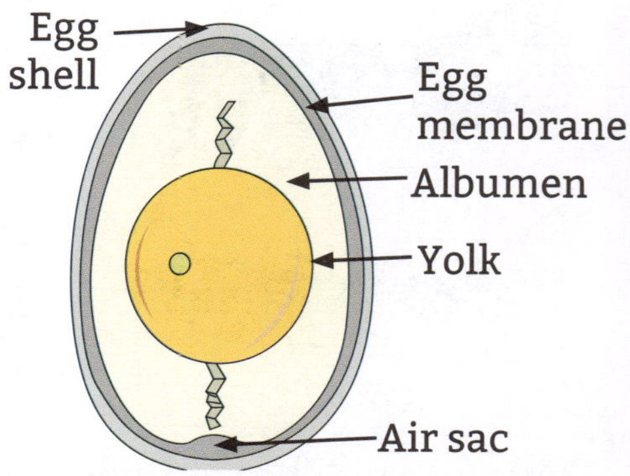

Structure of an egg

> **Science in Context**
>
> Yolk is rich in nutrients such as fats, minerals and vitamins; and albumen is rich in proteins.

The yolk consists of the essential nutrients required for the development of a growing baby called an **embryo**. The embryo ultimately develops into a young one.

The different stages of the development of an embryo into an adult are called the **life cycle** of an animal.

Life cycle of a hen

Fish

Fish lay plenty of eggs in water at a time. Out of these, only a few develop into baby fish as some of the eggs get eaten by larger fish and other animals. Generally, these eggs obtain warmth for incubation from the sunlight.

Frogs

Similar to fish, frogs also lay a large number of eggs in water. These eggs appear as large clusters of jelly-like substance known as **spawn**. The young ones that hatch from these eggs are called **tadpoles**. Tadpoles look very different from the adult frog. The process of the transformation of a young one into an adult that looks completely different is called **metamorphosis**. After metamorphosis, the tadpole becomes an adult frog.

Life cycle of a frog

Butterfly

The life cycle of a butterfly has four stages. Butterflies lay their eggs on leaves. A small worm-like **caterpillar** hatches from the eggs. This stage is called **larva**. The caterpillar grows in size by eating the leaves of the plants and develops a protective covering around itself. This stage is known as **pupa**. The pupa sheds its old skin many times. The process of shedding old skin by animals is called **moulting**. Finally, the adult butterfly comes out from the pupa.

Life cycle of a butterfly

Science in Context

Maggot is the larval form of a housefly. Wriggler is the larval form of a mosquito.

Grasshoppers and Cockroaches

The life cycle of grasshoppers and cockroaches involves three main stages. The tiny larvae that hatch from the eggs are called **nymphs**. The nymphs closely resemble their parent, but do not have wings. A nymph undergoes moulting several times and eventually develops into an adult.

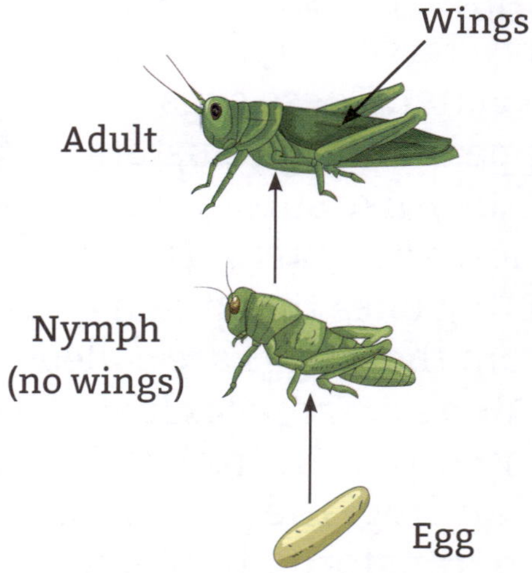

Life cycle of a grasshopper

Reptiles

Reptiles such as snakes and lizards lay their eggs on the ground. Out of these eggs, only a few develop into adults with the help of the sunlight that provide warmth to these eggs. Some of the eggs are eaten by other animals.

Revise and Recall

State whether the following statements are true (T) or false (F).

1. Lizards reproduce by laying eggs. ☐
2. The eggs produced by all the birds have the same kind of internal structure. ☐
3. Fish lay only one egg in water at a time. ☐
4. The young ones that hatch from the eggs of frogs are called pupa. ☐

ANIMALS THAT GIVE BIRTH TO BABIES

Animals that give birth to young ones and suckle[1] them with milk are called **mammals**. Dogs, cats, cows, monkeys, rabbits, elephants, kangaroos, giraffes, lions and human beings are examples of mammals.

The complete development of the young ones takes place inside the mother's body. The mother feeds the young ones with milk from her mammary glands after they are born.

Mammals have a well-developed brain. Most of them have hair on their body and most of them live on land. They breathe through their lungs. They are warm-blooded[2] animals.

Word Web

[1]**Suckle**: feed young ones with one's own milk

[2]**Warm-blooded:** maintain body heat even when the surrounding is cold or hot

Science in Context

Mammals are also called viviparous animals.

Wonder!

Bats are mammals even though they are able to fly like birds. Pouched mammals such as Kangaroo and Koala bear are called marsupials.

Kangaroo with its joey

Cow with its calf

Some mammals such as dolphins and whales live in water. They are called **aquatic mammals**. They do not have hair on their body. They breathe through lungs and often come up to the water surface to breathe in air. They give birth to young ones. Similar to land animals, the young ones are fed thick milk-like paste by their mothers.

Dolphin

Whale

Science in Context

Duckbilled platypus and spiny anteater reproduce by laying eggs. But they are still called mammals because they feed their young ones with their milk, have hair on their body and breathe through lungs.

Mammals Care for Their Young Ones

Mammals take care of their young ones for a long time. They keep their babies clean and warm. They feed their babies and protect them from enemies. Most fish, reptiles and insects do not take care of their young ones. They lay their eggs in a safe place and leave the young ones to live on their own.

Mammals care for their young ones

Wonder!

The *Tilapia* fish carries its eggs in its mouth until they hatch. The small fish hide in the parent's mouth when they are faced with danger.

Revise and Recall

State whether the following statements are true (T) or false (F).

1. In mammals, the complete development of the young ones takes place inside the mother's body. ☐
2. Mammals do not have well-developed brains. ☐
3. All mammals have hair on their body. ☐
4. Human beings do not take care of their young ones. ☐

Keywords

Incubation: The process of keeping eggs warm, often done by parent birds by sitting on them, until they hatch into young ones

Metamorphosis: The process of the transformation of a young one into an adult that looks completely different

Spawn: A cluster of eggs laid by a frog

Nymph: Larva of grasshoppers and cockroaches

Caterpillar: The larval stage of a butterfly

Moulting: The process of shedding old skin by animals

Mammals: Animals that give birth to young ones and suckle them with milk

Summary

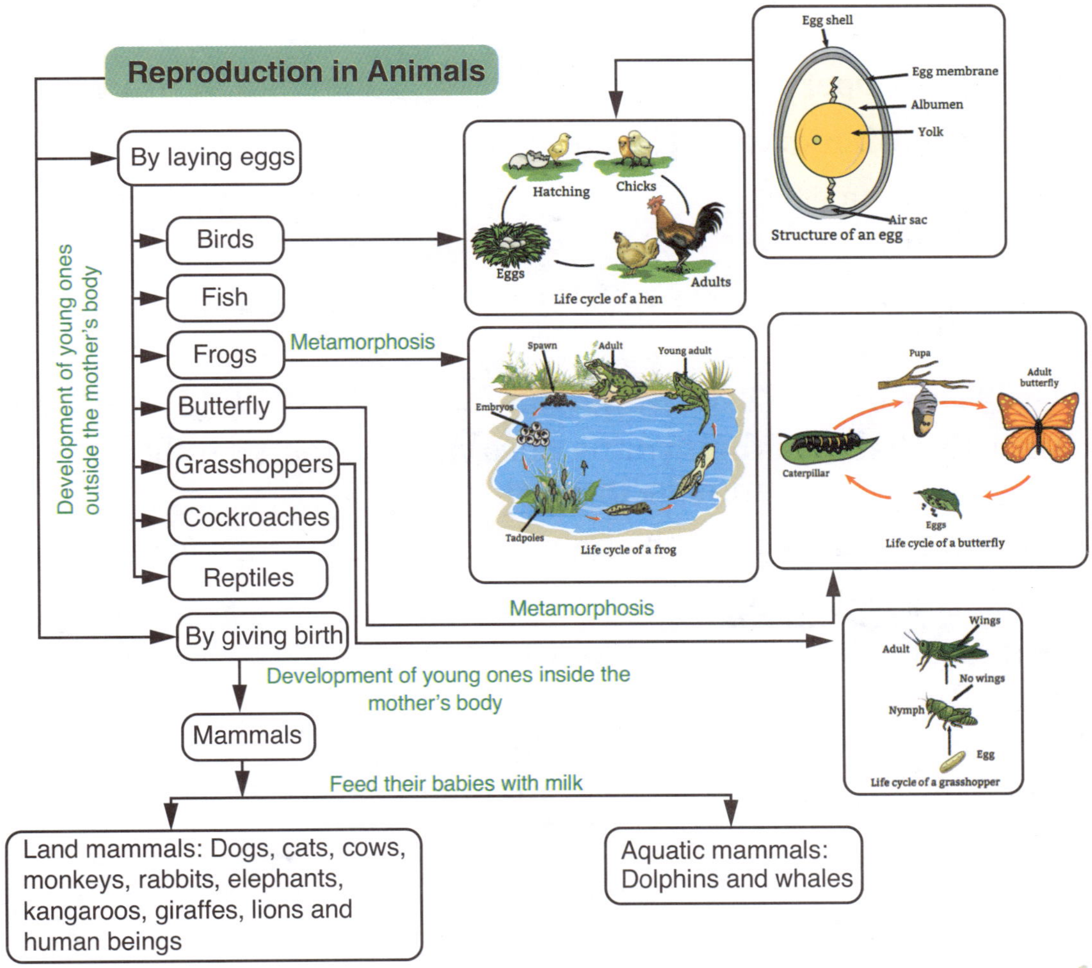

Exercise

W

A. Choose the correct option for each of the following. ia

1. Identify the animal that does not reproduce by laying eggs.
   (a) Housefly (b) Deer (c) Butterfly (d) Fish
2. The jelly-like white-coloured substance that is present inside the egg shell is
   (a) Albumen (b) Yolk (c) Egg shell (d) Embryo
3. The process of shedding old skin by animals is called
   (a) Incubation (b) Metamorphosis
   (c) Moulting (d) Life cycle
4. Identify the egg-laying animal from the following.
   (a) Hippopotamus (b) Zebra
   (c) Frog (d) Cat
5. In which of these animals, does the development of the young one take place inside the mother's body?
   (a) Grasshopper (b) Housefly (c) Rabbit (d) Lizard

B. Fill in the blanks with the correct words. ia

1. Birds reproduce by ______________. (laying eggs/giving birth to young ones)
2. The large cluster of frog's eggs is called ______________. (spawn/nymph)
3. Lizards lay their eggs ______________. (in water/on the ground)
4. Animals that feed their young ones with their own milk are called ______________. (mammals/insects)
5. Mammals breathe with the help of ______________. (skin/lungs)

C. Match the following.

	Column A		Column B
1.	Butterfly	(a)	Calf
2.	Hen	(b)	Caterpillar
3.	Frog	(c)	Tadpole
4.	Grasshopper	(d)	Chick
5.	Cow	(e)	Nymph

D. State whether the following statements are true (T) or false (F).

ia

1. All animals reproduce by laying eggs. ☐
2. Yolk is the yellow-coloured substance that is present inside the egg. ☐
3. Mammals such as dolphins come up to the surface of water to breathe in air. ☐
4. After hatching, the tiny caterpillar that comes out from the eggs of a butterfly is known as pupa. ☐
5. A tadpole looks similar to an adult frog. ☐

E. Give two examples for each of the following.

1. Egg-laying animals ____________ ____________
2. Animals that give birth to young ones ____________ ____________
3. Aquatic mammals ____________ ____________
4. Animals that lay eggs in water ____________ ____________
5. Animals that undergo moulting ____________ ____________

F. Give reasons for the following.

1. Eggs are kept under incubation.
2. The yolk of an egg is very important to the growing embryo.
3. Out of many eggs laid by snakes only a few develop into adults.
4. We say that frog undergoes metamorphosis.
5. Whale is considered as a mammal.

G. Answer the following questions briefly.

1. Define reproduction.
2. What are the different ways in which animals reproduce?
3. What is incubation?
4. What are aquatic mammals?
5. How do mammals take care of their young ones?

H. Answer the following questions.

1. Describe the structure of an egg with the help of a diagram.
2. Describe the life cycle of a butterfly.
3. What are the main features of mammals?

Cognitive Corner

Critical Thinking

1. Rahul says the young ones of all animals look like their parents. Do you agree? Why or why not?
2. A dolphin lives in water but does not have gills like other fish. Still, it survives in water. How?

Picture Study

Name the stages of the life cycle of a frog shown in the pictures given below.

______________ ______________ ______________

Project

1. Collect pictures of various animals from old newspapers and magazines. Group them as egg-laying animals and the animals that give birth to young ones. Paste these pictures in a scrapbook. Display your scrapbook in the classroom.
2. Take a chart paper and paste or draw various stages involved in the life cycle of a butterfly/frog/grasshopper. Write the description about each stage and display the chart in your classroom.

Life Skills

Put a tick mark (✓) against the correct statements and cross out (×) the wrong ones. Give reasons for your answer.

1. We should not pluck leaves or pull them unnecessarily. ☐
2. We should destroy or disturb birds' eggs. ☐
3. We should not throw waste in ponds. ☐
4. We should try to keep water and some grains or fruits in our balcony for birds. ☐

Worksheet

Nature has its own way of maintaining life on land. All living organisms reproduce to maintain life. In most cases, the young ones resemble their parents. However, in some cases, they do not resemble their parents such as tadpoles and frogs. Some babies at birth look different from their parents but over time, as they grow, they start resembling them. Nature is thus very colourful and unique.

Animals take care of their young ones until they can take care of themselves. It is us human beings that have caused harm by destroying the natural places they live in.

A. Have you seen a bird feeding its babies? How do you feel when you look at the little birds chirping and waiting for food from its parent?

____

____

____

____

B. Suppose a bird starts making nests in your garden or in your home, what would you do? Destroy it or let it continue? Why or why not?

____

____

____

____

C. There is a homeless puppy. It is looking for a home. You want to adopt it but your mother is not used to dogs. How would you convince your mother to adopt the puppy? Talk to her about the purpose of maintaining life on land and convince her. List down your reasons for adopting the puppy.

____

____

____

____

4 Animal Adaptations

Learning Checklist

- Adaptations to environment
- Adaptations for food
- Adaptations for protection
- Extinct and endangered animals

Let's Get Started

Look at the pictures of animals given below and identify the habitats they live in. Write in the space provided below each animal.

Land   Water   Tree

____________   ____________   ____________

Similar to plants, animals also undergo changes over a period of time to adapt to their surroundings. Let us learn about the adaptations of different animals in this chapter.

ADAPTATIONS TO ENVIRONMENT

a

Based on the environment in which they live, animals are grouped as terrestrial, aquatic, amphibian, aerial and arboreal.

Terrestrial Animals

Animals that live on land are called **terrestrial animals**. The climatic conditions on land vary from place to place.

Polar regions are extremely cold. Animals such as polar bears, Arctic foxes, penguins, seals and walruses live there. To protect themselves from the cold, these animals have thick, hairy skin. Animals such as polar bear and walrus also have a thick layer of fat under the skin called **blubber**.

Polar bear

Penguin

Due to the scarcity of food during cold periods, animals such as bear, frog and snake prefer to sleep throughout the winter and remain inactive. This long winter sleep is called **hibernation**.

Mountains are also very cold. Animals that live on mountains such as the mountain sheep, mountain goats and yaks have thick fur on their body, which keeps them warm during the cold weather. These animals have strong hooves[1] that help them to walk on the slopes of mountains.

Yak

Word Web

[1]**Hooves**: the hard covering present in the foot of some animals

Deserts are usually very hot. Animals that live in deserts such as camels have thick skin and less hair on their body. This helps to prevent water loss from their body.

Camel

Some animals such as snails, lizards and earthworms sleep for a long time during summer months to escape the heat. This long summer sleep is called **aestivation**.

Science in Context

A camel drinks a large amount of water at a time. Therefore, it can survive without water for long periods of time. The hump of the camel contains a large amount of stored fat. This is used when there is a scarcity of food. It has long legs and flat hooves, which help it to walk easily on the loose desert sand without the feet sinking in. A camel has double eyelids, which prevent the sand from entering its eyes. A camel is also called the ship of the desert.

Aquatic Animals

Animals that live in water are called **aquatic animals**. Fish, whale, turtle and octopus are a few examples of aquatic animals. Fish have fins, and whales and turtles have paddle-like flippers that help them in swimming. Most aquatic animals respire through gills.

Whale

Turtle

Amphibians

Animals such as frog and salamander that can live both in water and on land are called **amphibians**. Most amphibians have lungs that help them to breathe on land and moist skin that helps them to breathe underwater. Frogs have well-developed, strong hindlimbs that help them to hop on land and webbed feet to help them swim in water.

Frog

Aerial Animals

Animals that can fly and spend their maximum time in the air are called **aerial animals**. Birds are examples of aerial animals. They have hollow bones, boat-shaped body, wings and feathers to help them fly. Bats are the only mammals that can fly. Insects such as butterflies and dragonflies have thin, papery wings that help them to fly.

Bird

Arboreal Animals

Monkey

Koala bear

Animals that spend a majority of their time on trees are called **arboreal animals**. Monkeys, squirrels, tree lizards and koala bears are examples of arboreal animals. These animals have strong limbs and sharp claws that help them in climbing trees. The tail of monkeys helps them to hang onto the branches of trees.

Revise and Recall

State whether the following statements are true (T) or false (F).

1. Climatic condition on land is constant most of the time. ☐
2. Walruses have blubber. ☐
3. All aquatic animals respire through gills. ☐
4. Aerial animals have hollow bones. ☐
5. Tail helps a monkey to hang onto the branches of trees. ☐

ADAPTATIONS FOR FOOD

Based on the type of food that animals eat, they are grouped into herbivores, carnivores, omnivores, scavengers and parasites.

Herbivores

Deer

Animals that eat only plants are called **herbivores**. These animals have strong and broad teeth in the front called incisors to bite off leaves and grass; and strong chewing teeth with space in between them (for grinding) at the back. They travel long distances with the help of their long and strong legs in search of food. Examples include deer, giraffe and elephant.

Science in Context

Plant products are rich in a substance called cellulose. Human beings cannot digest cellulose. Most herbivores have microbes in their digestive tract that help them to digest cellulose.

Carnivores

Tiger

Animals that eat the flesh of other animals are called **carnivores**. These animals have pointed, sharp, long and curved canines to tear the flesh of their prey. Carnivores chew the flesh and bones with the help of broad and flat grinding teeth present at the back of their mouth. Examples include wolf, tiger and lion.

Omnivores

Crow

Animals such as bears, crows and human beings eat both plants and the flesh of other animals. They are called **omnivores**. They have all the three types of teeth except for birds.

Scavengers

Hyena

Animals that feed on dead and decaying animals are called **scavengers**. Examples include vultures, jackals, wild dogs and hyenas. Scavengers have sharp teeth for ripping and tearing flesh.

Parasites

Organisms that live on or inside the body of other living organisms and depend on them for food are called **parasites**. The animal on or inside which the parasite lives is called the **host**. Roundworms, hookworms and tapeworms are parasites that live inside the body of the host. Lice (*singular*: louse), ticks and fleas are parasites that live on the surface of the host's body. The mouth of these organisms is adapted to suck blood from the host's body.

Roundworm

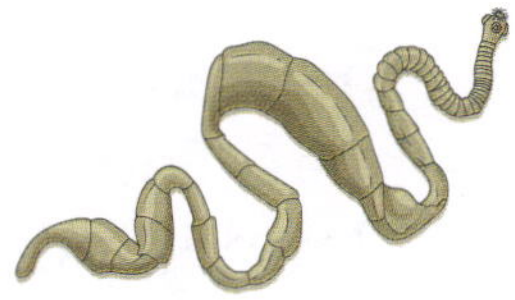
Tapeworm

Louse

Flea

ADAPTATIONS FOR PROTECTION

Animals show different types of adaptations to protect themselves from danger.

- Rabbits, deer, fish and mice can move very fast to protect themselves from their enemies.
- The thick skin of elephants and hippopotamuses helps in protecting them from the hot climate.
- Insects such as cockroaches have a hard outer body covering for protection.
- The hard shell of crabs and turtles protects their soft bodies.
- The sharp spines of porcupines protect them from their enemies.

The characteristics of animals (colour and shape) that help them to mix or merge with their surroundings are called **camouflage**. Most animals escape from their enemies or catch their prey by camouflaging themselves.

- Polar bears have white fur that blends with snow. It helps them to hide in snow.
- Some insects have the structure of a leaf (leaf insect) or a twig (stick insect) so that they can hide from their enemies.

Leaf insect

Stick insect

- Chameleons can change the colour of their skin. They change colour to actually warm up or cool down. Turning darker helps them to warm up their body because the dark colours absorb more heat. The change in colour also helps them to blend in with their surroundings.

Chameleon

EXTINCT AND ENDANGERED ANIMALS

Animals such as dodos, passenger pigeons, Caribbean monk seals and Tecopa pupfish are some of the species that are no longer found on the Earth. These animals are called **extinct animals**.

Dodo

Animals that are unable to adapt to their surroundings die and eventually become extinct. Millions of years ago, huge animals called dinosaurs lived on the Earth. When it became very cold, they were not able to adjust to the cold climate and became extinct.

Many animals are in danger due to the destruction of forests by human beings for their needs. The numbers of some animals such as tigers, cheetahs, giant pandas and Indian rhinoceros are fast declining and they may soon disappear completely from the Earth. These animals are called **endangered animals**.

Indian rhinoceros

Revise and Recall

State whether the following statements are true (T) or false (F).

1. Walrus is a terrestrial animal that lives in polar regions. ☐
2. Rabbit undergoes aestivation. ☐
3. Koala bear is an arboreal animal. ☐
4. Wolf is an omnivore. ☐
5. Roundworms live inside the body of the host. ☐

Keywords

Hibernation: The long sleep of animals during winter months

Aestivation: The long sleep of animals during summer months

Aerial animals: Animals that can fly and spend their maximum time in the air

Arboreal animals: Animals that spend a major part of their life on trees

Parasites: Organisms that live on or inside the body of other living organisms and depend on them for food

Camouflaging: The characteristics of animals (colour and shape) that help them to merge with their surroundings in order to escape from their enemies or to catch their prey

Extinct animals: Animals that are no longer found on the Earth

Endangered animals: Animals that are in danger of becoming extinct and may soon disappear

Summary

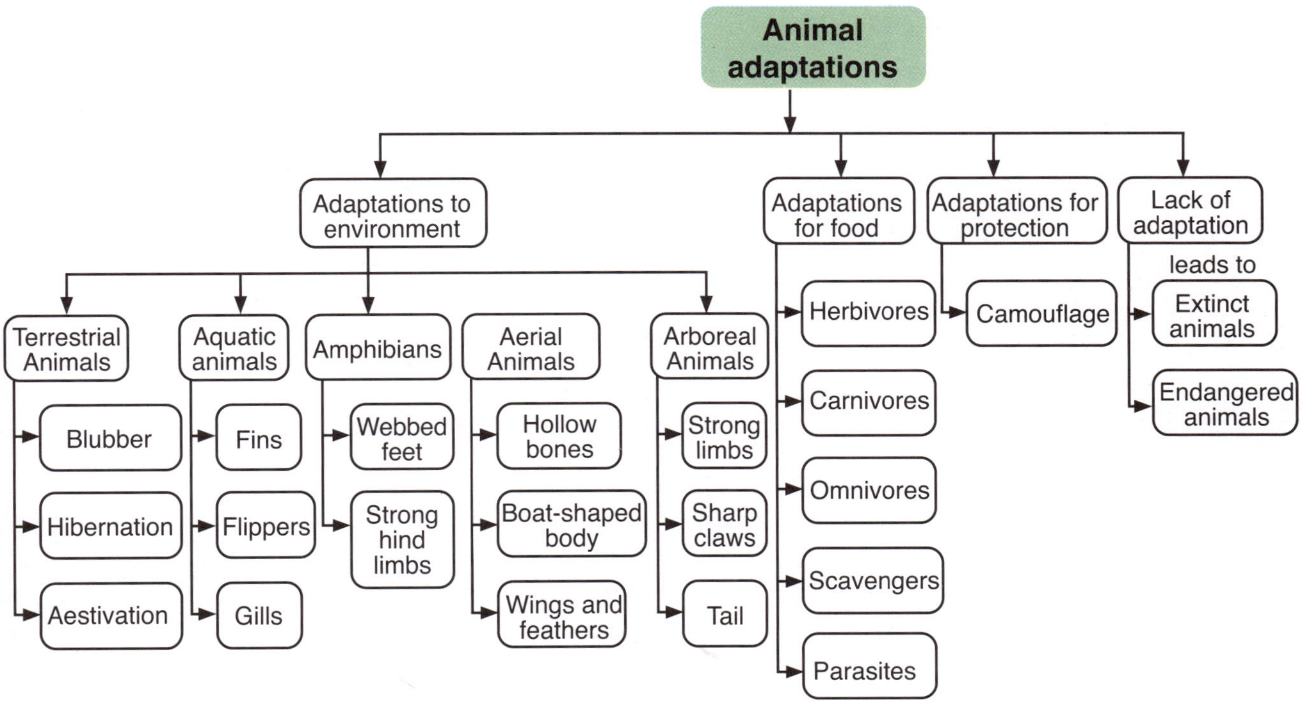

Exercise

W

A. Choose the correct option for each of the following. ia

1. Identify the animal that sleeps throughout the summer months.
   (a) Bear (b) Snail (c) Rabbit (d) Frog
2. Aquatic animals respire mostly through their
   (a) Skin (b) Lungs
   (c) Gills (d) Lungs and skin
3. Identify the parasite that lives on the host's body.
   (a) Roundworm (b) Hookworm (c) Lice (d) Tapeworm
4. Identify the animal that cannot protect itself by camouflaging.
   (a) Chameleon (b) Tiger
   (c) Hippopotamus (d) Polar bear
5. Identify the extinct animal from the following.
   (a) Giant panda (b) Indian rhinoceros
   (c) Dodo (d) Tiger

B. Fill in the blanks with the correct words. ia

1. A polar bear has ____________ to keep it warm. (blubber/flesh)
2. Winter sleep is also called ____________. (hibernation/aestivation)
3. Eagle is an example of an ____________ animal. (aerial/arboreal)
4. Koala bear is ____________ animal. (an arboreal/a terrestrial)
5. Crow is ____________. (a herbivore/an omnivore)

C. Match the following.

	Column A		**Column B**
1.	Deer	(a)	Aquatic animal
2.	Seal	(b)	Terrestrial animal
3.	Salamander	(c)	Arboreal
4.	Birds	(d)	Amphibian
5.	Koala bear	(e)	Aerial

D. State whether the following statements are true (T) or false (F).

1. All terrestrial animals undergo aestivation. ☐
2. The thick fur of the yak helps in protecting it from the cold weather. ☐

3. Insects such as butterflies have thin, papery wings that help them to fly. ☐
4. Amphibians breathe through lungs as well as moist skin. ☐
5. A bear is an example of a herbivore. ☐

E. Give two examples for each of the following.

1. Arboreal animals ____________ ____________
2. Animals that undergo hibernation ____________ ____________
3. Carnivores ____________ ____________
4. Scavengers ____________ ____________
5. Parasites that live inside the host's body ____________ ____________

F. Give reasons for the following.

1. Mountain sheep have thick fur on their body.
2. Camels have thick skin and thin hair.
3. Chameleon changes the colour of its skin.
4. Tigers have sharp, curved canines.
5. Dodo is no longer found on the Earth.

G. Answer the following questions briefly.

1. Why do some animals undergo hibernation?
2. Mention the adaptations shown by arboreal animals.
3. Distinguish between parasites and scavengers.
4. Define camouflage.
5. How are extinct animals different from endangered animals?

H. Answer the following questions.

1. Describe in brief about the various adaptations of terrestrial animals.
2. Describe the adaptations of aquatic animals and amphibians.
3. Describe in brief about the grouping of animals according to their eating habits.
4. Describe the various adaptations shown by animals for their protection.

Cognitive Corner

Critical Thinking

1. How is a camel different from a yak even though both are terrestrial animals?
2. Why do we need to protect the endangered animals?
3. Why does a frog lay its eggs in water?

Picture Study

Look at the pictures shown below and circle the odd one out. Give reasons for your selection.

1.    

2.    

Project

1. Collect pictures of various animals from old newspapers and magazines. Group them according to their habitat as terrestrial, aquatic, amphibian, aerial and arboreal animals, and paste the pictures in a scrapbook. Write a few lines about the adaptations shown by the animals in each habitat. Display your scrapbook in the classroom.
2. Make a chart on animals living in different habitats. Collect pictures of the animals given below. Make a table as shown and paste the pictures under the correct column.

   Fish, Cow, Horse, Monkey, Tiger, Flying squirrel, Bird, Polar bear, Penguin, Seal, Koala bear, Camel, Lizard, Whale, Tree lizard

Terrestrial Animals	Aquatic Animals	Aerial	Arboreal Animals

3. Make a model of a polar bear using paper.

Materials required: Chart paper, crayons/markers, glue, scissors, paper bag and thread/string

Procedure:

a. Take an empty paper bag.

b. Carefully fold the edges of the paper bag along the dotted line as shown below to get the shape of a polar bear's head.

c. Take a chart paper and with the help of scissors, cut small eyes, ears, paws and claws of the polar bear.

d. Paste them in the relevant places using glue.

e. With the help of markers/crayons, draw the mouth and nose on the polar bear's head.

f. Make a small hole at the centre of the paper bag and attach a thread/ string to hang it on the wall.

Your paper polar bear is ready.

Life Skills

Which of the following images shows the correct way of treating animals? Put a tick mark (✓) against the correct actions and cross (×) against the wrong ones. Give reasons for your answer.

Worksheet

A weaver bird building its nest

Of all the wonderful creatures, great and small, that roam this Earth, birds have a special place in everyone's hearts. Their songs as they go about their daily routines, or their majestic flying powers, all these fill us with wonder.

To survive on the Earth, they show different adaptations. To attract a female bird, some male birds build amazing nests while some others are prettier and more attractive than females. Cocks have combs on their heads, peacocks have beautiful feathers and so on. However, they too need to camouflage to avoid their enemies who might want to kill them, their eggs or their young ones.

A. Pictures of three birds are given below. Identify which ones have adapted to camouflage themselves and which ones have adapted to attract females.

A frigatebird

____

A tawny frogmouth

____

Lesser bird of paradise

____

B. Why do we need to protect these amazing birds? How can we protect them? Write a slogan for protecting these amazing birds.

____

____

____

____

____

____

____

5 Circulatory System and Excretory System

Learning Checklist

- Circulatory system
- Excretory system

Let's Get Started

Our body has different organs. According to their functions, organs are grouped into different organ systems. In Class 3, you have learned about the circulatory and excretory systems in brief. Can you recall the names of the organs that make up the circulatory and excretory systems? Complete the charts given below.

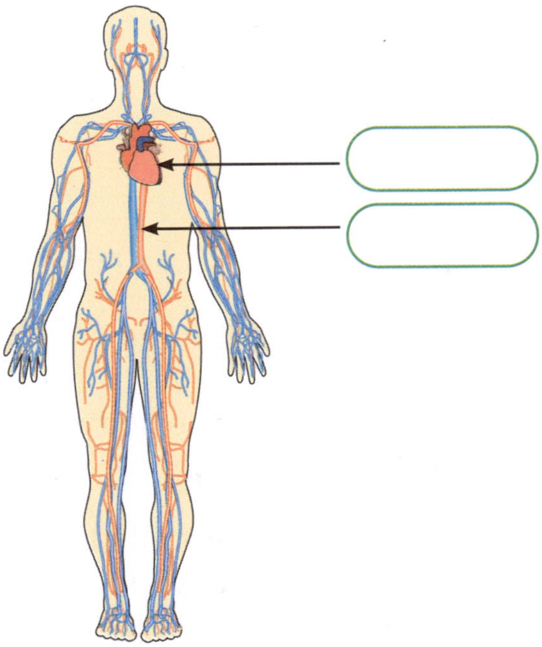

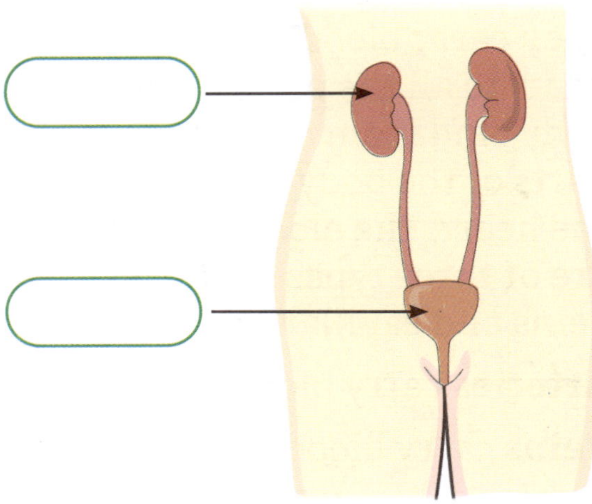

In this chapter, we will learn more about the organs and functions of the circulatory and excretory systems.

CIRCULATORY SYSTEM

a

The circulatory system transports substances inside our body. It consists of the heart, a network of blood vessels and blood.

Heart: The heart is a muscular organ that pumps blood into the larger blood vessels, which branch into smaller ones to reach all the organs of a human body. The heart also receives blood from all the organs of the body.

Blood vessels: These are thin tube-like structures that start from the heart and run through the entire body forming a network. They carry blood from the heart to all the parts of the body, and from different parts of the body back to the heart. The blood vessels are of three types—arteries, veins and capillaries.

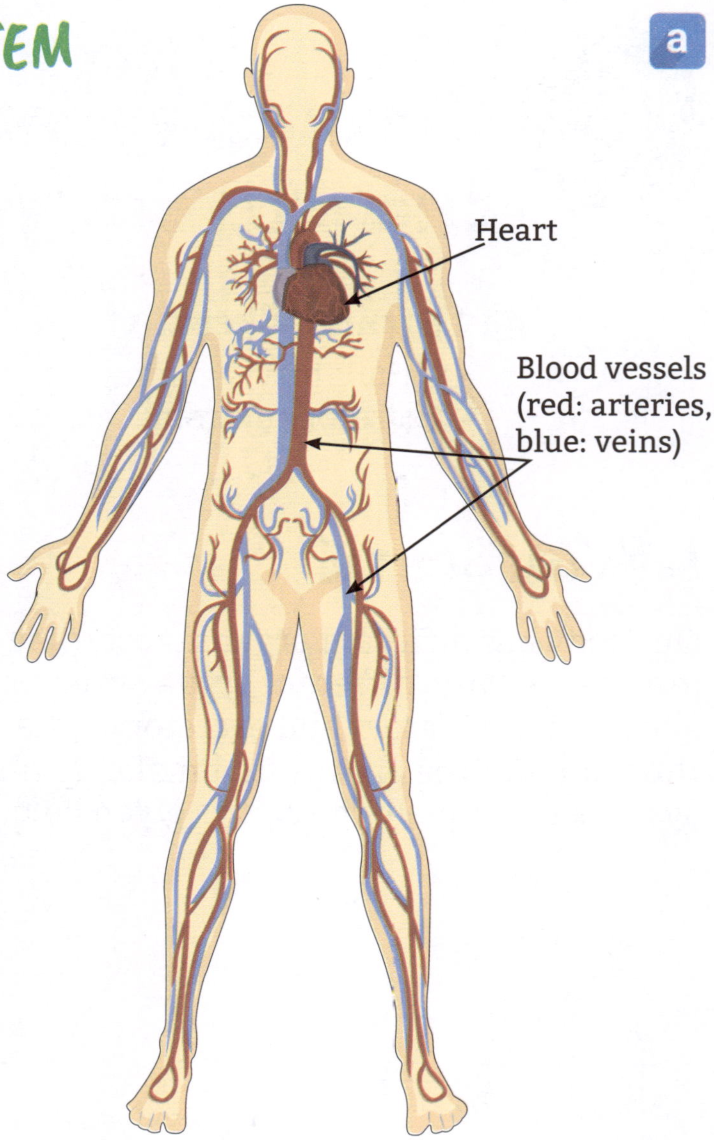

Human circulatory system

Arteries carry blood from the heart to different parts of the body.

Veins carry blood from different parts of the body to the heart.

Arteries branch out into smaller and thinner blood vessels called arterioles. These further branch into even smaller blood vessels called **capillaries**. Capillaries are the smallest blood vessels. Many capillaries reunite to form veins. Capillaries help in the exchange of gases, water and nutrients between the blood and the tissues.

Blood: Blood is a red-coloured fluid that flows through the blood vessels from the heart to all the parts of the body and then back to the heart. It transports nutrients absorbed from food, oxygen, carbon dioxide and water inside the body. It also transports the waste products produced in the body to the excretory system so that they can be removed from the body.

Revise and Recall

Who am I?

1. I am a muscular organ that pumps blood. ____________
2. I carry blood from the heart to all parts of the body and then back to the heart. ____________
3. I am the smallest blood vessel. ____________
4. I am the blood vessel that carries blood from the heart to different parts of the body. ____________
5. I am the blood vessel that carries blood from different parts of the body back to the heart. ____________
6. I flow through the blood vessels. ____________

EXCRETORY SYSTEM

The excretory system removes wastes from our body. The organs of the excretory system include a pair of kidneys, a pair of tubes called ureters, a urinary bladder and a urethra.

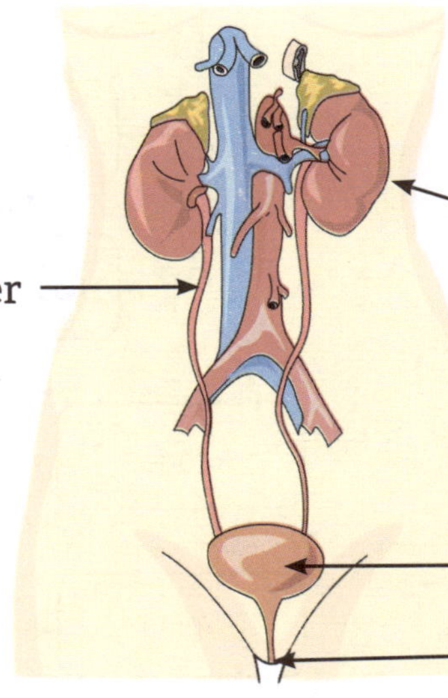

Human excretory system

Kidneys are bean-shaped structures that act like filters to collect harmful wastes such as urine and excess salts from the blood. **Ureters** are a pair of tubes that carry these wastes from the kidneys to the urinary bladder. **Urinary bladder** stores the urine until it is released from the body. **Urethra** is a tube that lets the urine in the urinary bladder pass out of the body.

Keywords

Circulatory system: The organ system that helps to transport substances to different parts of our body

Excretory system: The organ system that helps to remove wastes from our body

Summary

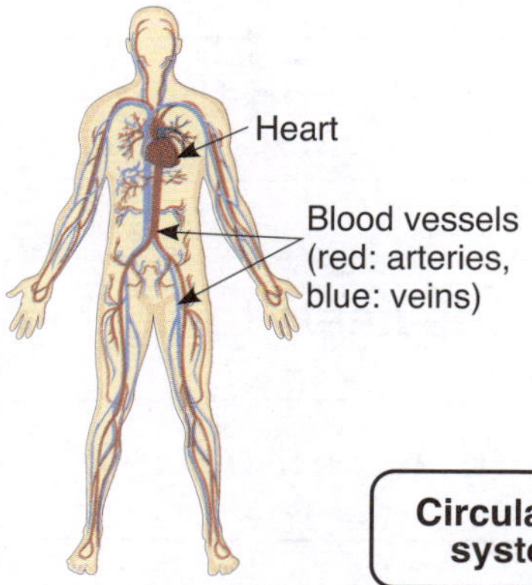

Human circulatory system

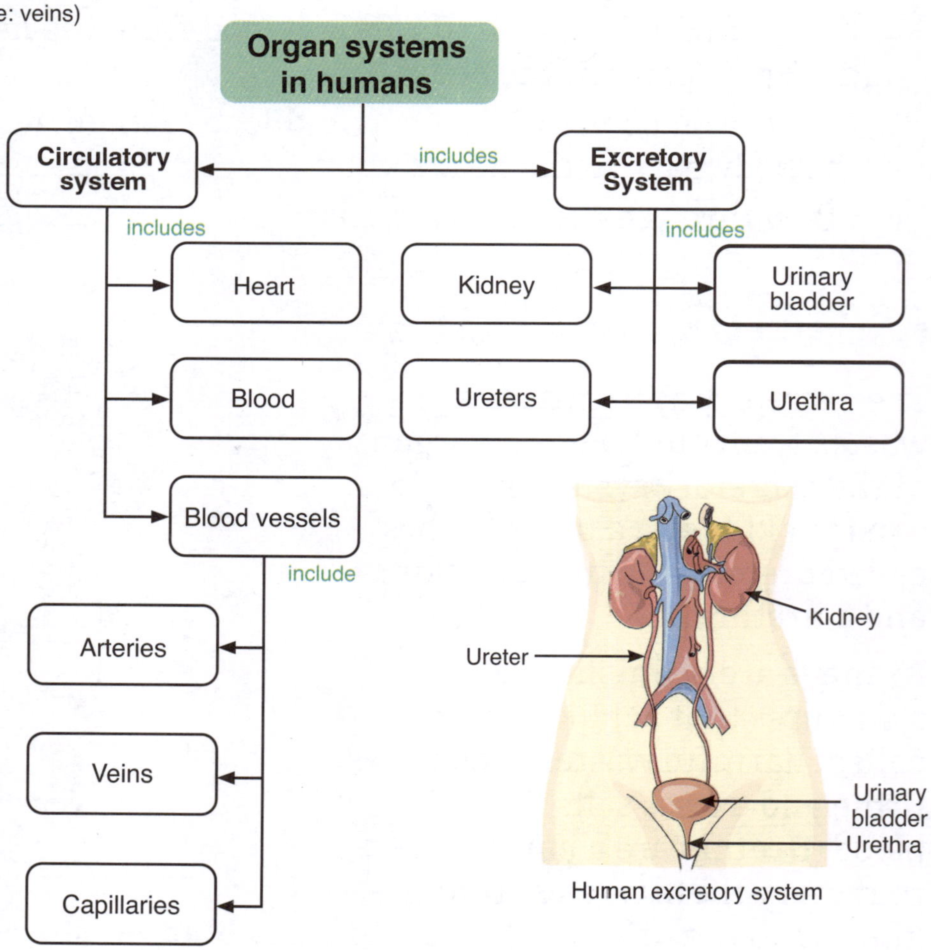

Human excretory system

Exercise

W

A. Choose the correct option for each of the following. ia

1. Which of these is a type of blood vessel?
   (a) Veins (b) Capillaries
   (c) Arteries (d) All of these
2. This blood vessel carries blood from the different parts of the body to the heart.
   (a) Artery (b) Vein (c) Capillary (d) Ureter
3. The function of the excretory system is to remove
   (a) saliva (b) waste (c) blood (d) water
4. Which of these is an organ of the excretory system?
   (a) Blood vessel (b) Urinary bladder
   (c) Heart (d) Blood
5. Ureters carry wastes from the
   (a) Kidneys to the blood vessel (b) Heart to the blood vessel
   (c) Kidneys to the urinary bladder (d) Urinary bladder to the kidneys

B. Fill in the blanks with the correct words. ia

1. The heart pumps ____________ to all the organs. (wastes/blood)
2. The ____________ system removes wastes from the body. (excretory/circulatory)
3. ____________ filter waste from the body. (Heart/Kidneys)
4. ____________ are the tubes that connect the kidneys to the urinary bladder. (Urethra/Ureters)
5. Urine gets stored in the ____________. (urinary bladder/kidneys)

C. Match the following.

	Column A		**Column B**
1.	Kidneys	(a)	A pair of tubes
2.	Blood vessels	(b)	Red-coloured fluid
3.	Blood	(c)	Muscular organ
4.	Heart	(d)	Bean-shaped
5.	Ureters	(e)	Network of thin tubes

D. State whether the following statements are true (T) or false (F). ia

1. Circulatory system removes wastes in the form of urine from the body. ☐
2. The heart pumps blood into the blood vessels. ☐
3. Blood vessels carry blood to only the hands and legs in the body. ☐
4. Our body has only one kidney. ☐
5. Kidneys act as a filter to remove wastes from the body. ☐

E. Name the following in one word. ia

1. The smallest of all blood vessels ____________________
2. Blood vessels that carry blood from different organs back to the heart ____________________
3. Bean-shaped structures that act like filters to collect harmful wastes ____________________
4. The tubes that carry wastes from the kidneys to the urinary bladder ____________________
5. The body part where urine is stored ____________________

F. Give reasons for the following.

1. The urinary bladder is an important organ of the excretory system.
2. A network of thin blood vessels are found through out the body.
3. Capillaries form the junction between arteries and veins.
4. Excretory system is essential in a body.
5. Blood is considered as the medium of circulation in body.

G. Answer the following questions briefly.

1. Name the organs of the circulatory system.
2. What is the role of kidney in our body?
3. Name the three types of blood vessels.
4. Name the organs of the excretory system.

H. Answer the following questions.

1. Write a note on blood vessels.
2. Describe the organs and functions of the human excretory system with the help of a diagram.

Cognitive Corner

Critical Thinking

1. Why does your heart beat faster when you exercise?
2. What would happen if we did not have an excretory system?

Picture Study

Label the parts of the organ system shown below and also name the organ system.

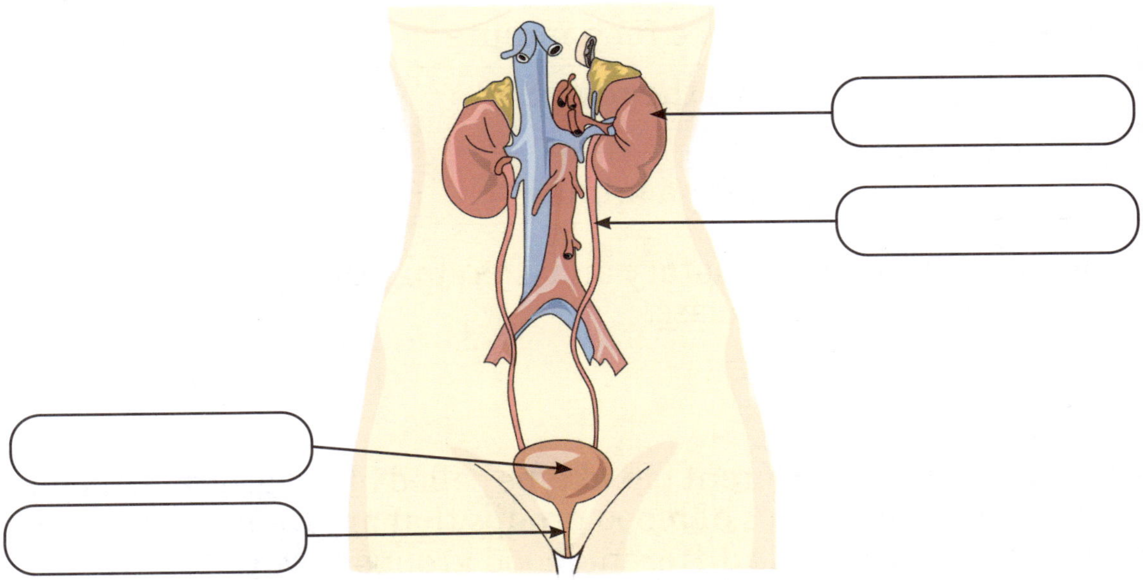

Name of the organ system:

____

Project

1. The number of times a heart beats in a minute is called the heart rate or pulse. We can feel the pulse in our body at those places where an artery passes close to the skin.

   Feel your pulse by placing two fingers on your wrist as shown in the picture given alongside.

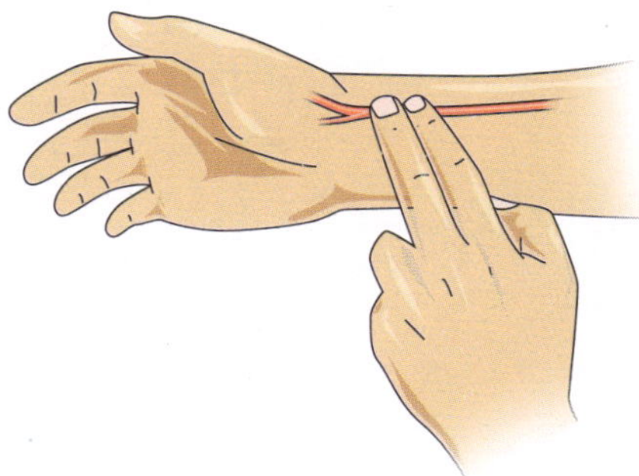

When we do some physical activity such as exercise, more blood has to be sent to the muscles and the heart rate increases.

Carry out the activities given in the table and count your heart rate after each activity. Fill in the boxes and observe how fast your heart beats after performing these actions.

Action	Heart Rate
Sitting	
After marching for a minute	
After jogging in one place for a minute	
After walking around the room for a minute	
After lying down for a minute	

2. Draw the human circulatory and excretory systems on a chart, and display it in your class.

Life Skills

Every person has a different blood type called blood group. Find out about the different types of blood groups that are found in human beings. Make a list of the different blood groups in your family and find out with whom your blood group matches. Now, have you heard about blood donation? How is the knowledge of blood group related to blood donation? Find out and discuss the same with your classmates.

9 INDUSTRY, INNOVATION AND INFRASTRUCTURE

Worksheet

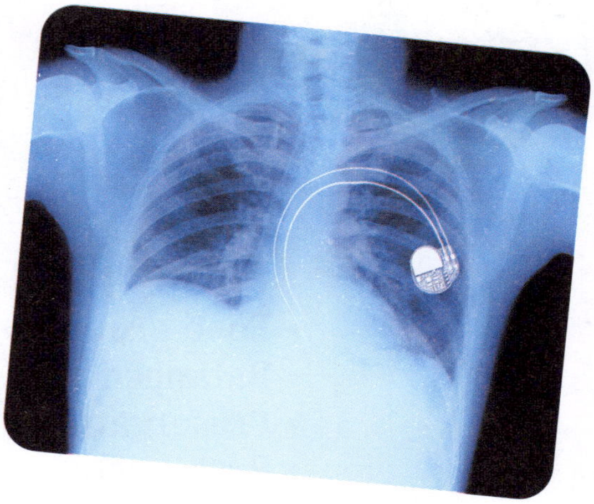

From birth until death, the heart pumps blood tirelessly through our bodies. This blood carries fresh oxygen from our lungs to every part of our body. It is this oxygen that gives us energy from the food we eat.

However, sometimes with age, the heart muscles become weak. The heart normally beats 72 times in a minute. If a heart becomes weak, then it loses its pumping power and the number of beats per minute reduces. So, a person with a weak heart may faint now and then, from the lack of oxygen to their brain.

Nowadays, medical science has developed a technology to help such weak hearts. Just like a cell that makes a watch tick, a device, called a pacemaker, helps the heart pump when it stops. Whenever the number of heartbeats comes down below a certain level, the pacemaker delivers a tiny electric current to the heart, making it pump.

A. What are the two main things we should do in our lives to have a healthy heart?

____

____

____

____

____

____

B. Find out the names of other devices that help a human body work properly.

____

____

____

____

____

____

6 Food: Our Basic Need

Learning Checklist

- Food groups
- Balanced diet
- Preservation of food
- Rest, posture and exercise

Let's Get Started

Sort the following food items into plant and animal products, and fill in the table given below.

Butter

Dried grapes

Bread

Ghee

Maize

Cashew nuts

Pepper powder

Fish fry

Plant products	Animal products

WHY DO WE NEED FOOD?

In our day-to-day life, we do many activities such as going to school, studying, playing, going for a walk, dancing, swimming, etc. To do these activities, we need energy. Where do we get energy from?

Food gives us the energy to do our daily activities. We should eat healthy food in order to stay fit.

Walking

Dancing

FOOD GROUPS

Substances present in food that help the body to grow and stay healthy are called **nutrients**. The main nutrients found in food are carbohydrates, proteins, fats, vitamins and minerals. Food also contains roughage and water. Based on what nutrients the food contains, they are grouped into three food groups: energy-giving food, body-building food and protective food.

Carbohydrates

Carbohydrates are known as **energy-giving food**. There are two types of carbohydrates present in food—sugar and starch. Wheat, rice, potato and sweet potato contain starch. Food items such as pastries and bananas contain sugar.

Carbohydrates

People who do more physical work need more energy. Therefore, an athlete needs more carbohydrates in his diet than a person who sits and works in an office all day.

Proteins

Proteins help in the growth of the body and the repair of worn-out tissues and cells. They build our muscles too. Hence, proteins are known as **body-building food**. Growing children need more proteins than adults. Food items such as milk, cheese, egg, fish, meat and pulses contain proteins.

Proteins

Science in Context

Lack of protein in the diet causes a deficiency disorder called kwashiorkor.

Fats

Fats are present in food items such as oil, butter, *ghee*, cream, cheese, *paneer* and nuts. Fats are also energy-giving food. They provide more energy than carbohydrates. Our body needs fat in very small amounts. Consumption of excess fat is not good for health as they get stored in the body and increase the body weight.

Butter

Cream

Oil

Cheese

Vitamins and Minerals

Our body requires vitamins and minerals in very small quantities. Vitamins and minerals help us to stay healthy and protect us from diseases. Hence, they are known as **protective food**.

Eggs

Fruits and vegetables

Fresh fruits, leafy vegetables, pulses, cereals and milk are some important sources of vitamins and minerals.

Milk

Pulses

Cereals

Minerals such as iron and calcium are required to keep our body healthy and strong.

Calcium makes bones and teeth strong. Milk, curd and nuts are some of the calcium-rich foods.

Lack of iron in our body makes us feel tired and weak. Green leafy vegetables, oranges and apples are some of the iron-rich foods.

To get minerals, we should eat vegetables, fruits, egg, fish, milk, salt and cereals.

Roughage and Water

Roughage is the fibre present in some green vegetables, fruits, cereals, etc. It cannot be digested and does not provide any nutrient to our body, but it helps in the movement of food through the intestines and in the removal of wastes from the body.

Water is very important for our body. It helps in digestion and maintains the body temperature. Our body loses water through sweat, breath and urine. In order to make up for this loss, we should drink plenty of water every day.

BALANCED DIET

a

A balanced diet is a meal that contains carbohydrates, proteins, fats, vitamins, minerals, water and fibre in the right proportion[1]. To stay healthy, we should always have a balanced diet.

Word Web

[1]**Proportion**: amount

Revise and Recall

State whether the following statements are true (T) or false (F).

1. Carbohydrates are known as energy-giving food. ☐
2. Consumption of fat in excess is good for health. ☐
3. Vitamins are known as body-building food. ☐
4. Roughage is the fibre present in the food. ☐
5. To stay healthy, we should not drink water. ☐

PRESERVATION OF FOOD

Cooked or uncooked food gets spoilt when it is kept exposed to air and moisture for a long time. The process of treating food to prevent it from getting spoilt is called **preservation**.

Some ways of preserving food are given below:

- **Refrigerating**: Keeping fruits, vegetables and cooked food in the fridge prevents them from getting spoilt.
- **Drying**: In this method, water is completely removed from the food item. One simple way is to dry the food item under the sun. For example, dates and raisins are preserved as dry fruits.
- **Canning**: The moisture in the air can spoil food. Hence, food can be kept in airtight containers to prevent them from getting affected by moisture. For example, beans, tomatoes and chillies.
- **Pickling (using salt)**: Salt and oil forms a concentrated solution that is used to preserve pickles. For example, mango or chilly pickle.
- **Jellying (using sugar)**: Keeping fruits or vegetables in sugar syrups is one of the ways of preserving food. For example, mixed fruit jam.

Refrigerating

Drying

Canning

Pickling

Jellying

REST, POSTURE AND EXERCISE

In addition to a balanced diet, sufficient amount of rest, a good posture and regular exercise are essential to stay healthy.

Rest

Resting

Rest is very important for the body. We need at least 6 to 8 hours of sleep in a day. Lack of sleep makes us feel tired and it can also make us fall sick.

Posture

Posture is the position in which we keep our body while standing, sitting or walking. Having a correct posture helps us in many ways:

- Our bones and muscles stay healthy.
- We do not get tired quickly.
- We do not get backaches and muscle cramps.
- We look good.

Sitting Standing

Exercise

Regular exercise such as running, walking, cycling and playing different sports helps us to stay healthy and fit. Nowadays, yoga has also become a popular form of exercise.

If we exercise regularly, then

- our bones and muscles get stronger.
- we sleep well.
- we do not feel tired.
- we have more energy to work.

Exercising

Keywords

Nutrients: Substances present in food that help the body to grow and stay healthy

Roughage: The fibre present in green vegetables, fruits and cereals

Balanced diet: A meal that contains carbohydrates, proteins, fats, vitamins, minerals, water and fibre in the right proportion

Preservation: The process of treating food to prevent it from getting spoilt

Summary

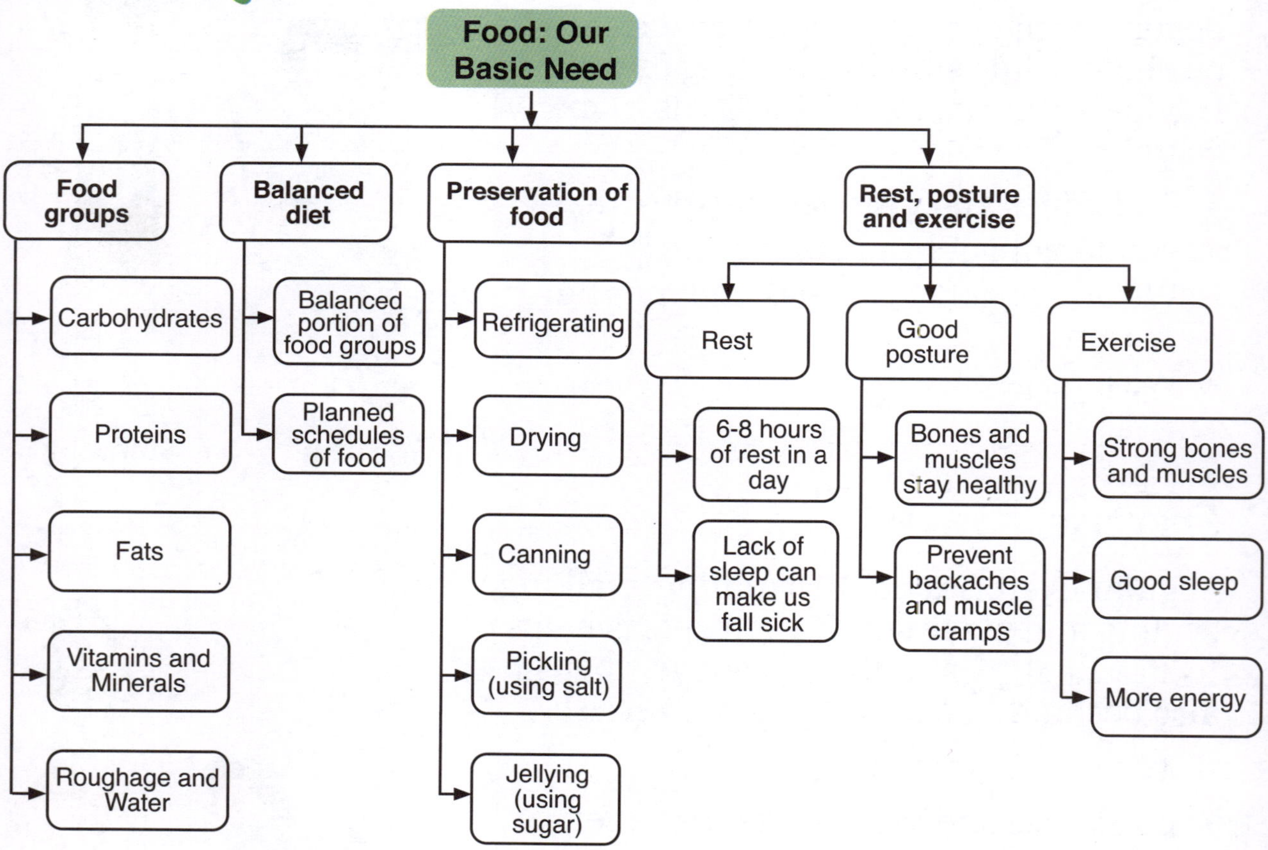

Exercise

W

A. Choose the correct option for each of the following. ia

1. Which of these is essential for people who do more physical work?
   (a) Proteins (b) Carbohydrates
   (c) Vitamins (d) Roughage
2. Proteins are also known as
   (a) Iron-rich food (b) Body-building food
   (c) Fibre-rich food (d) None of these
3. Which of these, when eaten in excess, will increase the body weight?
   (a) Fats (b) Proteins (c) Carbohydrates (d) Vitamins
4. Drying is a method of preserving food by
   (a) Adding salt (b) Adding sugar
   (c) Freezing (d) Removing water
5. Posture refers to the body's
   (a) Position (b) Bones
   (c) Muscles (d) None of these

B. Fill in the blanks with the correct words. ia

1. Food contains ______________, which help us to grow and stay healthy. (nutrients/preservatives)
2. Food items that are rich in ______________ are called energy-giving foods. (carbohydrates/vitamins)
3. Oil, butter, *ghee*, cream and cheese are rich in ______________ . (proteins/fats)
4. Roughage is the ______________ present in some green vegetables, fruits and cereals. (fibre/nutrient)
5. The process of treating food to prevent it from getting spoilt is called ______________ . (balanced diet/preservation)

C. Match the following. ia

Column A	**Column B**
1. Carbohydrates	(a) Prevent diseases
2. Fat	(b) Prevents food from getting spoilt
3. Vitamins	(c) Helps in the formation of bones and teeth
4. Preservation	(d) Butter
5. Calcium	(e) Potato and sweet potato

D. Name the following.

1. The diet that contains all the nutrients in the right proportion ____________
2. Position of the body while standing, sitting or walking ____________
3. The fibre present in some green vegetables, fruits and cereals ____________
4. Substances in food that help the body to grow and stay healthy ____________

E. Give reasons for the following.

1. Our body needs fats in small amounts.
2. One should not skip eating roughage in their diet.
3. Tomatoes can be stored in air-tight containers.
4. We must include fruits and vegetables in our diet.
5. Exercising regularly is a good practice.

F. Answer the following questions briefly.

1. What are carbohydrates?
2. Why do athletes need more carbohydrates than a person sitting in office?
3. What is the role of roughage?
4. Why is water essential in our diet?
5. What is a balanced diet?

G. Answer the following questions.

1. Name the different food groups. Explain proteins and vitamins with examples.
2. Name the different ways of preserving food and give examples for each.
3. How does a correct posture help us?

Cognitive Corner

Critical Thinking

1. Food does not get spoilt quickly in winter as compared to summer. Why?
2. Renu falls sick very often. Which food items should she eat to prevent from falling sick?

Picture Study

Write B for body-building foods, E for energy-giving foods and P for protective foods.

Project

1. What do you eat regularly? List the names in a table as shown below. Find out the nutrients present in these food items.

Name of the Food Items	Name of the Nutrients Present
Rice and *rasam*	

2. Special food items are prepared during festivals. Some of the famous food items are given below. Unscramble the words to identify the names of the dishes.

Dishes	Answers	Religious Festivals
MLPU AKCE (two words)		Christmas
EESWT KLMI (two words)		Diwali
EERKH		Ramzan

Life Skills

Often, the tasty food we eat contains less nutrients and more fat. (Example: Deep fried items such as potato chips.) We should avoid eating such food items on a regular basis.

Make a list of five food items that you should avoid eating or eat in very small amounts. Also, give reason why those food items should be avoided or eaten in very small amounts.

3 GOOD HEALTH AND WELL-BEING

Worksheet

In the past, food was usually cooked at home and people ate out to celebrate special days. Nowadays, most families have both parents who are working. It is easier to buy food which is available in packs. It can be easily prepared at home. People living alone also find it easier to buy and cook processed food. They do not have to buy items separately and spend a lot of time cooking them.

However, having a lot of processed food is harmful for our health. To preserve food for a long time, certain chemicals are added which are not healthy. Processed foods do not supply the desired amount of vitamins and minerals needed by our body. This can lead to a lot of diseases such as diabetes, high blood pressure and obesity.

Draw a poster on 'Healthy Food Habits' to show why we should have home-made food as much as possible.

7 Digestion of Food

Learning Checklist

- Structure and types of teeth
- Care of teeth
- Digestive system
- Microbes

Let's Get Started

Teeth help us to bite and chew the food we eat. They also help us to speak. Clean and white teeth give us a beautiful smile. Teeth can be healthy only if they are taken good care of.

Put a tick mark (✓) against the things you do to take care of your teeth.

1. Brush twice daily ☐
2. Have milk daily ☐
3. Eat chocolates daily ☐
4. Visit a dentist regularly ☐

In this chapter, we will learn about the types of teeth, and how teeth and other organs in our body help in the breakdown of food.

TEETH

A newborn baby does not have any teeth; it starts developing teeth when it is six months old. This first set of teeth is called the **milk teeth**. Milk teeth are about 20 in number.

> **Science in Context**
>
> Some people have only 28 teeth in the permanent set of teeth. The remaining 4 teeth appear later during the age of 17–21 and are called **wisdom teeth**. Some people do not have wisdom teeth at all!

Between the age of 6 and 12, the milk teeth begin to fall off one by one. Hence, the milk teeth are also called the temporary teeth. New teeth start growing in their places. This second set of teeth is called the **permanent teeth**. There are 32 permanent teeth in total, 16 in the upper jaw and 16 in the lower jaw. The permanent teeth last until old age.

Structure of Teeth

a

A tooth has three parts: crown, neck and root.

Crown: The visible part of the tooth above the gums is called the crown.

Neck: The part of the tooth below the crown touching the gums is called the neck.

Root: The part of the tooth inside the gums is called the root.

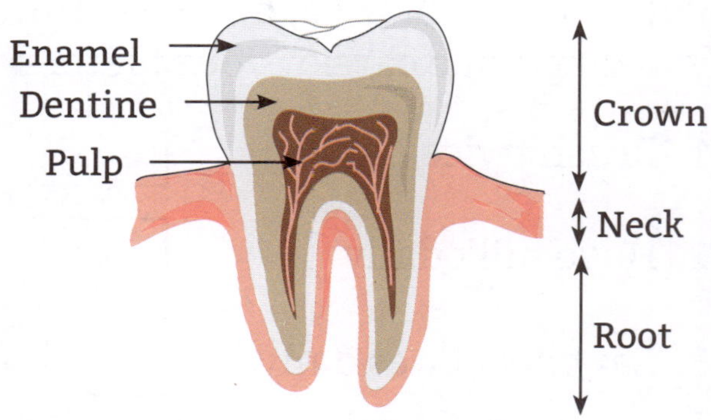

Structure of a tooth

The hard, white outer covering of a tooth is called the **enamel**. Enamel is the hardest part of our body.

There is another layer below the enamel called the **dentine**. Below the dentine lies the pulp. Dentine offers support to the enamel and conveys impulses from enamel to the pulp and root. **Pulp** is the soft part of the tooth. It has blood vessels and nerves inside it, which are connected to the gums. The nerves in the pulp send messages to the brain.

Types of Teeth

a

Teeth are mainly classified into four types based on their functions: incisors, canines, premolars and molars.

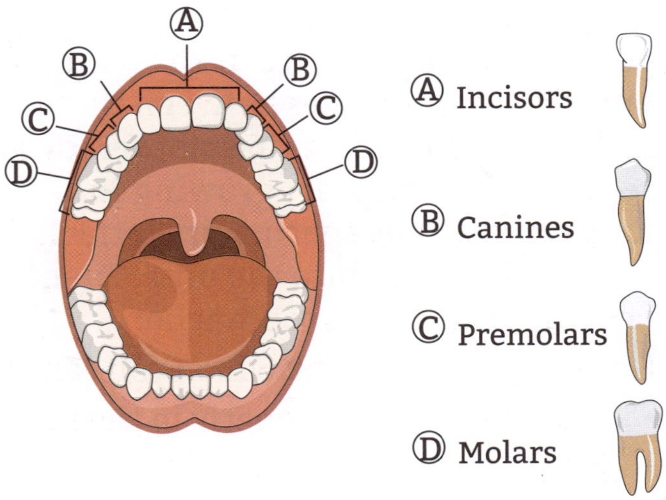

Incisors

These teeth help in cutting and biting off pieces of food. There are four incisors in the upper jaw and four in the lower jaw. They are placed in the front in both the jaws.

Canines

These teeth are seen on either side of the incisors in both the upper and lower jaws. They help in holding and tearing the food. There are a total of four canines, two in the upper jaw and two in the lower jaw. Carnivores have canines that are longer and sharper as they are modified to tear flesh faster and with ease.

Premolars

These teeth help in crushing and grinding the food. There are four premolars each in the upper and lower jaws. They are found next to the canines. These teeth are usually broader than other types of teeth.

Molars

These teeth are found towards the back of the mouth. They help in chewing and grinding the food. There are 12 molars in total, six in the lower jaw and six in the upper jaw. These teeth grow at different stages. They are bigger and broader than other teeth.

Science in Context

Herbivores use incisors to bite off the leaves from plants, and molars to grind the bitten off leaves.

CARE OF TEETH

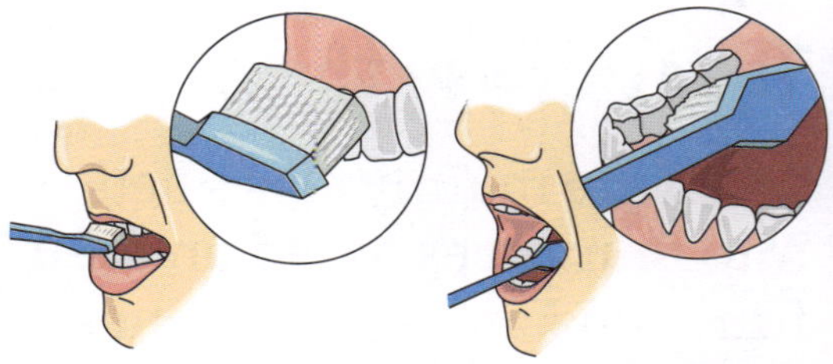

Teeth should be brushed properly to keep them healthy

When we eat food, tiny food particles get stuck to the surface of the teeth and also in the spaces between them. If these food particles are not removed regularly, germs start growing in these areas. These germs first attack the enamel, then the dentine and finally move into the pulp. Eventually, the germs attack the nerves, resulting in toothache.

Here are a few ways by which you can keep your teeth clean and healthy:

- Brush your teeth properly in the morning and at night before going to bed. Moving your toothbrush upwards and downwards in a circular motion is the right way to brush your teeth. You should brush the inner and outer surfaces of teeth and also on the sides of teeth.
- Gargle[1] and rinse your mouth after every meal.
- Use a mouthwash and dental floss[2], if possible.
- Avoid eating too many candies and chocolates.
- Eat lots of salads and fruits.
- Drink milk and eat food items that are rich in calcium such as cheese, eggs, etc.
- Visit a dentist[3] regularly to know how healthy your teeth are and get them treated, if required.

Word Web

[1]**Gargle**: clean the mouth and throat with water or a mouthwash

[2]**Dental floss**: a soft thread used for cleaning the spaces between the teeth

[3]**Dentist**: a person qualified to treat people suffering with tooth problems

Revise and Recall

Put a tick (✓) against the correct statements and cross (×) against the wrong ones.

I can take care of my teeth by:

1. Brushing them only once a day. ☐
2. Eating only chocolates. ☐
3. Gargling my mouth after every meal. ☐
4. Visiting the dentist only when I have a toothache. ☐

DIGESTIVE SYSTEM

Our body gets energy from the food we eat. To get energy, food has to be broken down into smaller substances that can be easily absorbed by the body. The process of the breakdown of food into smaller particles that can be easily absorbed by the body is called **digestion.**

The organs that help in the process of digestion make up the **digestive system**. The figure given alongside shows the human digestive system.

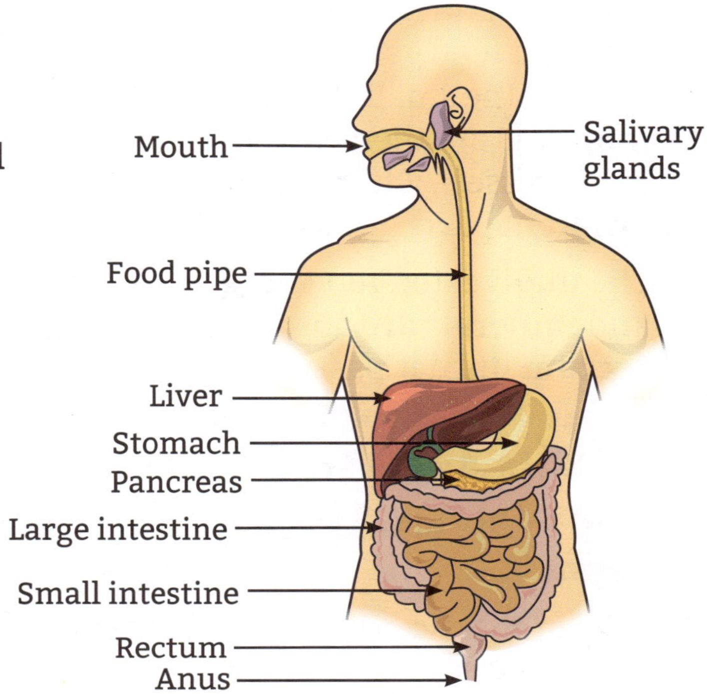

Human digestive system

Process of Digestion

Digestion of the food we eat starts in the **mouth**. The teeth bite and chew the food into smaller pieces. Saliva is a digestive juice secreted in the mouth by structures called **salivary glands**.

Saliva mixes with the food and makes it soft, moist and easy to swallow. The soft and moist food is now called the **bolus**. Food that contains starch, such as rice, is broken down into sugar by the saliva and hence tastes sweet.

The bolus then enters the **food pipe**. The food pipe moves by contracting and relaxing alternatively. This movement helps in pushing the food down into the **stomach**. It is a sac-like organ where the food is churned, physically breaking it down into smaller particles. This process takes several hours. Stomach produces acid and digestive juices that help to digest the food.

From the stomach, the remaining undigested food is pushed into a long coiled tube called the **small intestine**. Here, the digestive juices produced by the small intestine, the **liver** and the **pancreas** mix with the food and digest it.

All the useful nutrients from the digested food get absorbed by the walls of the small intestine. These nutrients are then absorbed by the blood vessels, which carry them to different parts of the body.

Science in Context

The rumbling sound in your stomach occurs when there is no food in the stomach and the stomach and intestines contract.

The undigested food enters the **large intestine** where the extra water and minerals are absorbed. The remaining solid waste is stored in the **rectum** until it passes out from the body through the **anus**.

Revise and Recall

Fill in the blanks using the names of the organs of the digestive system.

From the mouth, the food enters the ________________ and then passes into the ________________. From the stomach, the digested food then moves into a long coiled tube called the ________________. The food is completely digested as the juices from the ________________, ________________ and ________________ also mix with the food. The undigested food passes into the ________________ where the extra water and minerals are absorbed. The remaining solid waste is stored in the ________________ until it passes out of the body through the ________________.

MICROBES

Microbes are tiny living beings that cannot be seen with the naked eye. They can only be seen under a microscope[1]. They can be found everywhere: in food, soil, water and even inside and outside our body.

Word Web

[1]**Microscope**: an instrument that makes very small objects appear big

The main categories of microbes are bacteria, viruses, fungi and protozoa.

Bacteria

Bacteria (*singular*: bacterium) are made up of only one cell. They can be of different shapes such as rod shaped, round or spiral.

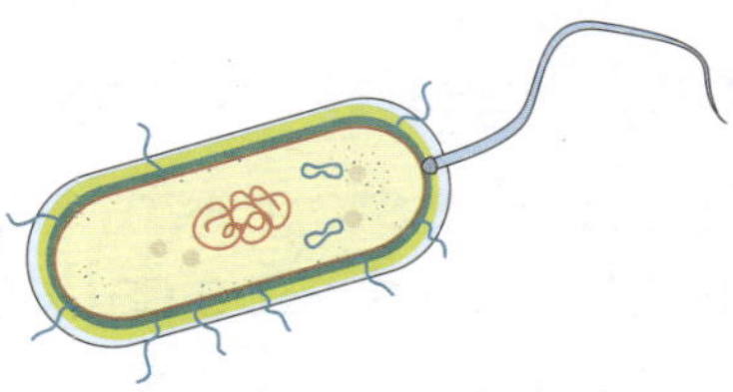

A bacterium

Viruses

Viruses (*singular*: virus) are the smallest living beings that can only be seen under a very powerful microscope.

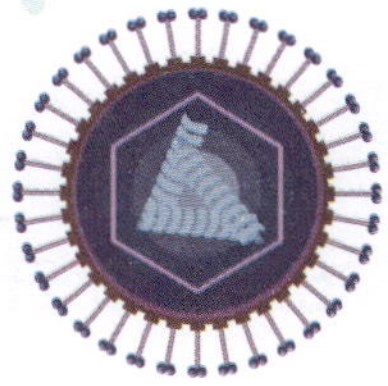

A virus

Fungi

Fungi (*singular*: fungus; *pronounced*: fuhng·gee) are the microbes that grow mainly on dead and decaying matter.

Fungi

Protozoa

Protozoa (*singular*: protozoan) are single-celled microbes.

Useful microbes

Some microbes are useful to us. Useful microbes help us in the following ways:

- Bacteria help in changing milk into curd.
- Bacteria and fungi help in breaking down dead matter.
- Protozoa are used as soil fertilizers.
- Fungi such as yeast help in making bread.
- Some bacteria help in digesting the food we eat.
- We obtain medicines from some bacteria and viruses.

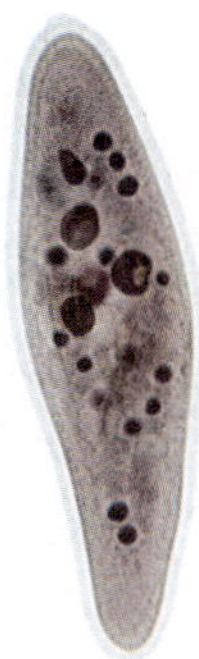

A protozoan

Harmful microbes

Some microbes are harmful to us and cause diseases. These microbes are called **germs** or **pathogens**.

- Bacteria cause diseases such as typhoid, tetanus and cholera.
- Viruses cause diseases such as flu, chicken pox, dengue, mumps and even common cold.
- Fungi mainly cause skin diseases such as ringworm, candidiasis and athlete's foot.
- Protozoa cause diseases such as dysentery and malaria.

Science in Context

The pandemic COVID-19, that started in late 2019, is caused by a new virus called the SARS-CoV-2.

Keywords

Crown: The visible part of the tooth above the gums

Enamel: The hard, white outer covering of a tooth

Dentine: The part of a tooth found below the enamel

Pulp: The soft part of a tooth that has blood vessels and nerves inside it

Digestion: The process of the breakdown of food into smaller particles that can be easily absorbed by the body

Digestive system: The organ system that helps in the process of digestion

Microbes: Tiny living beings that can only be seen under a microscope

Summary

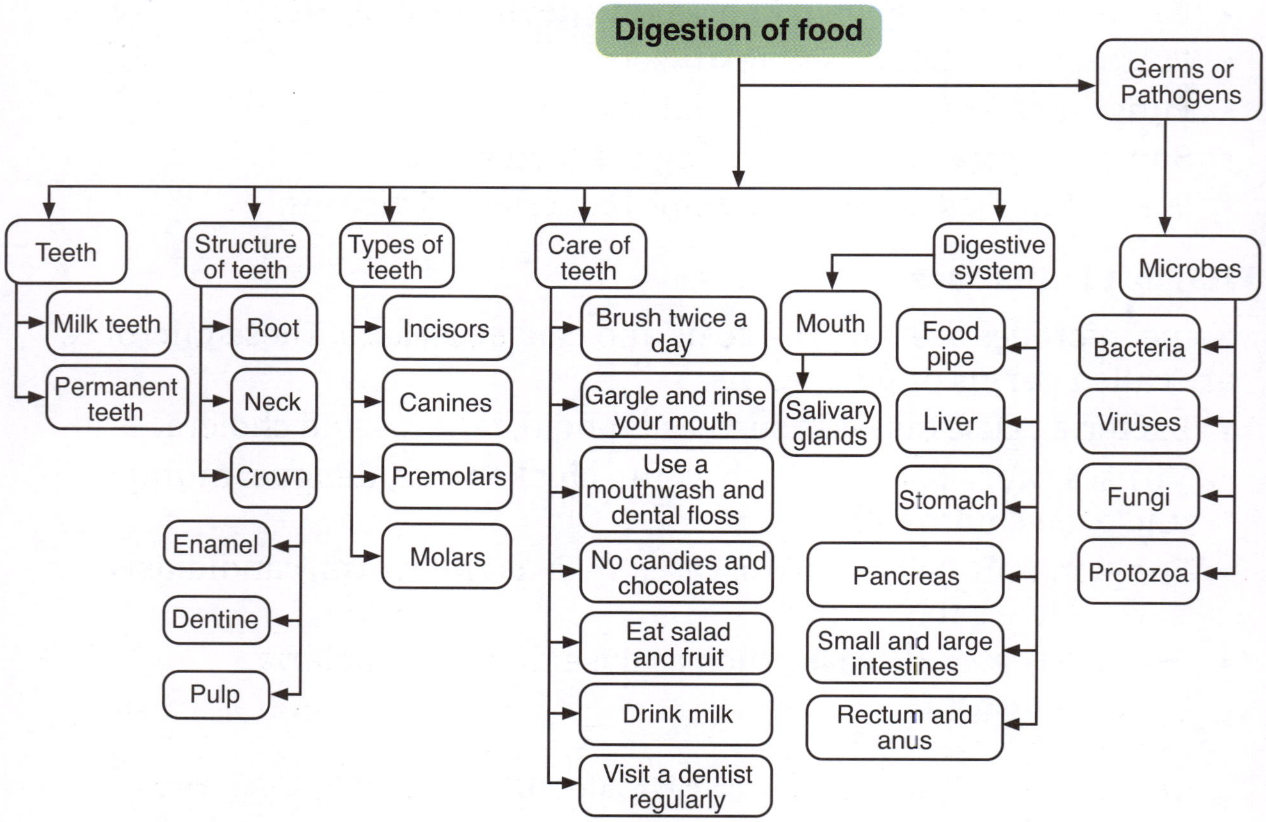

Exercise

W

A. Choose the correct option for each of the following. ia

1. The teeth that help in holding and tearing the food are
   (a) Incisors (b) Canines (c) Premolars (d) Molars
2. Toothache can be avoided by
   (a) Eating very little sweets
   (b) Brushing teeth regularly
   (c) Eating lots of salads and drinking lots of milk
   (d) All of these
3. The organ(s) of the digestive system is/are
   (a) Pancreas (b) Large intestine
   (c) Liver (d) All of these
4. The organ that produces acid and digestive juices to digest food is
   (a) Liver (b) Intestine (c) Stomach (d) Food pipe
5. The microbes that can be of different shapes are
   (a) Bacteria (b) Protozoa (c) Viruses (d) Fungi

B. Fill in the blanks with the correct words. ia

1. There are __________ teeth in the permanent set. (16/32)
2. The part of the tooth inside the gums is called the __________. (crown/root)
3. From the stomach, the remaining undigested food is pushed into a long coiled tube called the __________. (small intestine/large intestine)
4. __________ grow mainly on dead and decaying matter. (Fungi/Viruses)
5. Typhoid and tetanus are caused by __________. (protozoa/bacteria)

C. Match the following. ia

	Column A		**Column B**
1.	Bacteria	(a)	Athlete's foot
2.	Pathogens	(b)	Common cold
3.	Virus	(c)	Malaria
4.	Protozoa	(d)	Harmful microbes
5.	Fungi	(e)	Cholera

D. State whether the following statements are true (T) or false (F).

ia

1. Milk teeth are formed after the permanent teeth fall off. ☐
2. Digestion is the breaking down of food into smaller particles. ☐
3. Saliva is a digestive juice secreted in the mouth. ☐
4. The undigested food is stored in the stomach. ☐
5. Microbes cannot be seen with the naked eye. ☐

E. Answer the following in one word.

ia

1. The first set of teeth ________
2. The hard, white outer covering of the tooth ________
3. The structures in the mouth that produce saliva ________
4. Tiny living beings that can only be seen under a microscope ________
5. Microbes that help in making bread ________

F. Give reasons for the following.

1. Milk teeth are also called temporary teeth.
2. Carnivores have longer and sharper canines.
3. Rice tastes sweet when chewed.
4. Drinking milk is good for teeth.
5. Microbes cannot be seen with the naked eye.

G. Answer the following questions briefly.

1. Name the parts of a tooth.
2. List the organs of the digestive system.
3. What is the function of the stomach in the digestive system?
4. What are germs? Give an example.
5. What are the different shapes of bacteria?

H. Answer the following questions.

1. Describe the structure of a tooth with the help of a diagram.
2. Name the different types of teeth and write their functions.
3. List four ways by which we can take care of our teeth.
4. How are microbes useful to us?

Cognitive Corner

Critical Thinking

1. Richa, who is 12 years old, has 14 teeth in her upper jaw. Her father, who is 40 years old, has 16 teeth in his upper jaw. Can you explain why?
2. Kriti often swallows food without chewing it properly. Is it a good practice? Why or why not?

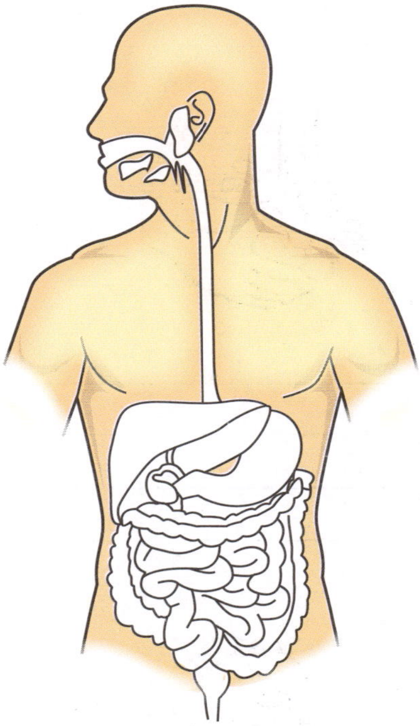

Picture Study

Use different crayons to colour the organs of the digestive system. Label each organ.

Project

Create a life-sized model of a human body. Draw cut-outs of the different body organs using a chart paper. Then assemble the organs to create the model.

Life Skills

Join the happy tooth with the action that makes it healthy and happy. One has been done for you. How will you keep your teeth healthy and happy?

I will drink a lot of milk.

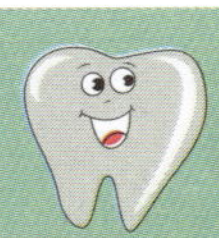

Happy tooth

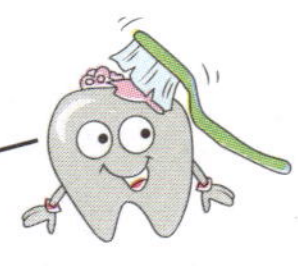

I will brush regularly.

I will brush my teeth only sometimes.

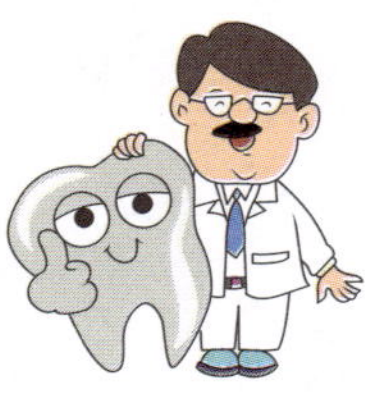

I will visit my dentist.

I will eat lots of candies and chocolates.

I will eat lots of salads and fruits.

Worksheet

Germs are tiny living beings that enter our bodies and cause diseases. They enter our bodies through the air we breathe, the food we eat or the water we drink.

To prevent germs from entering our bodies, we should be clean and maintain good habits.

Look at the pictures and write which good habit is being shown. Write a caption for each habit.

TO REMAIN HEALTHY

8 Clothes

Learning Checklist

- Need for clothes
- Fibres and fabrics
- Care of clothes

Let's Get Started

Look at the pictures given below. Choose the words from the box and write the name of each piece of clothing in the space provided.

Trousers	Raincoat	Muffler	Boots

1.  ______________

2. 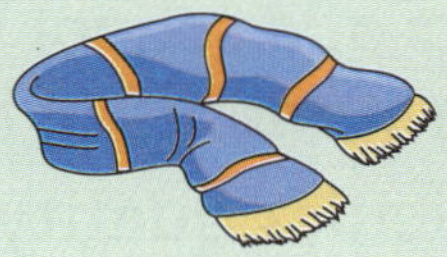 ______________

3.  ______________

4. 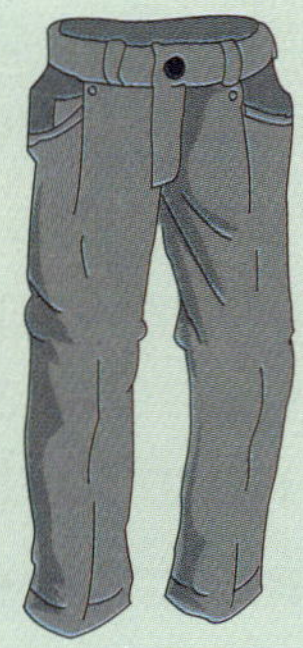 ______________

Do you know when these clothes are worn? Write a sentence on each.

1. ____
2. ____
3. ____
4. ____

NEED FOR CLOTHES

Clothes are also one of our basic needs like food and shelter. Early humans used to cover their bodies with leaves or barks of trees and skins of dead animals. As time progressed, human beings learned how to weave and stitch, and started wearing stitched clothes.

An early human

Importance of Clothes

Let us look at the importance of clothes in our daily life.

- **Protection:** Clothes protect our body from extreme weather conditions. It absorbs sweat, prevents chills and acts as a buffer between our body and protects us from the external climate. It also provides protection against burns and scratches that might happen due to accidents. We wear raincoats during monsoon, cotton clothes in summer and woollen clothes in winter.

A firefighter

- **Safety:** Certain types of clothing are worn to protect ourselves from injury. For example, firefighters wear asbestos clothing which do not catch fire, a cyclist wears a helmet, police officers wear bullet proof vests.
- **Uniforms:** Porters, postmen, lawyers, doctors and soldiers wear special clothes for work. These clothes tell us what work they do and are called *uniforms*. Students of a school have a specific uniform differentiating them from students of other schools.
- **Sanitation:** Clothes made of a particular quality prevents infection and contamination. Surgeons wear specific clothes such as gloves, aprons, caps and face masks to avoid contamination.
- **Identification:** Certain types of clothes are specific to certain places. In India, each state has its own traditional wear. The clothes worn by people living in Kashmir, North-East India and Kerala are different because the weather in these regions is different. Clothes also represent the culture of that place.

Clothes worn in Kashmir

Clothes worn in Kerala

FIBRES AND FABRICS

a

Fibres are long, thin, hair-like threads that can be made into a fabric by weaving[1] or knitting[2]. Fibres can be natural or man-made. Once the fabric is made, it is stitched to make clothes.

Weaving

Knitting

Word Web

[1]**Weaving**: a method by which fabrics are made by crossing two or more fibres or threads together

[2]**Knitting**: a method by which a clothing is made by interlocking loops of a single or more long threads

Natural Fibres

Fibres obtained from natural sources such as plants and animals are called **natural fibres**. For example, we get cotton, jute and linen from plants and wool and silk from animals.

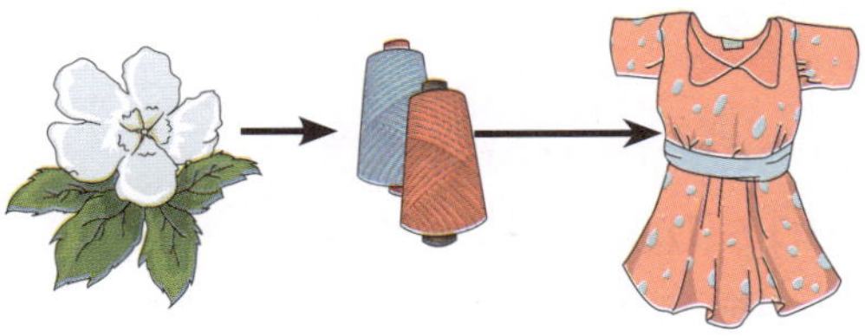

Cotton materials from cotton plant

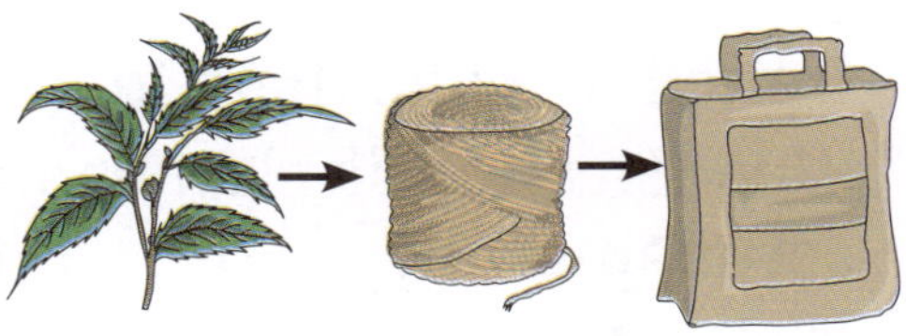

Jute materials from jute plant

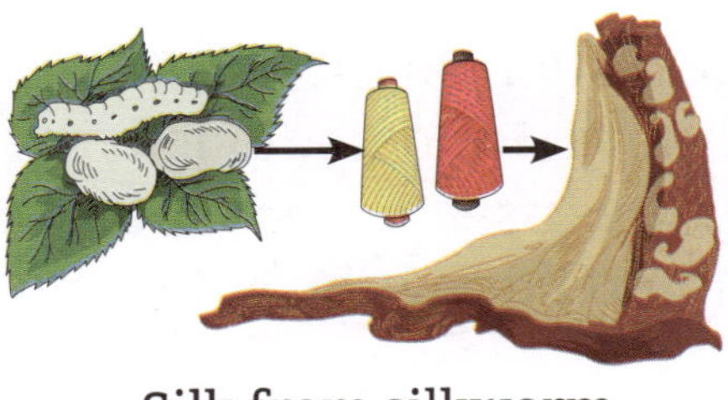

Silk from silkworm

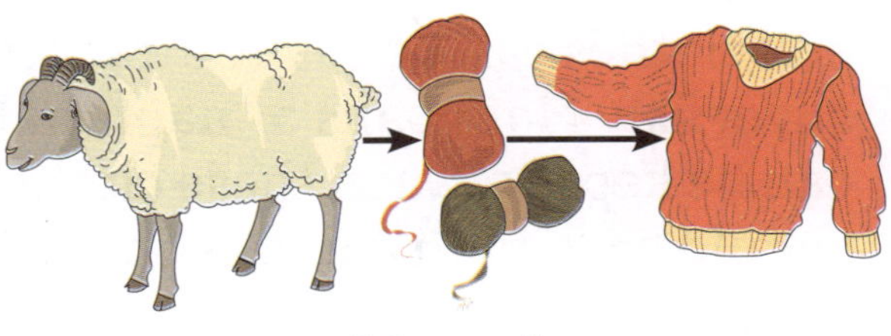

Wool from sheep

Science in Context

The cultivation of silkworm for producing silk is known as sericulture.

Synthetic or Man-made Fibres

Polyester clothes

Terylene jacket

Fibres that are not found in nature but are made by human beings are called **synthetic** or **man-made fibres**. Nylon, polyester, terylene and rayon are some examples of synthetic fibres.

Synthetic fibres are strong and they last long. Their colours do not fade; they can be stretched easily, are waterproof and wrinkle-free.

CARE OF CLOTHES

It is important to know about the fibre from which our clothes are made so that we can take proper care of them.

- Clothes should be washed properly with a soap or detergent to remove dirt, stains and sweat. Wearing clean clothes helps us to stay healthy.
- After washing, clothes should be dried properly.
- Clothes may have wrinkles after washing. So, they should be ironed to make them look neat.
- Woollen and silk clothes should be washed gently, without scrubbing. They should be dried in mild sunlight or dry-cleaned. We should not soak woollen or silk clothes in hot water as it may damage the fabric.
- Clothes should be stored properly when not in use. Woollen and silk clothes can be easily attacked by insects such as moth and silverfish. Moth balls or naphthalene balls and dried neem leaves can be kept between these clothes to keep the insects away. Clothes should be kept in clean cupboards and should be regularly taken out and dried under the sun.

Ironing

Storing clothes properly

Naphthalene balls kept between clothes

Revise and Recall

Fill in the blanks with the correct words.

1. Early humans used to cover their body with ___________. (animal skins/cotton fabric)
2. Clothes that tell us what work we do are called __________. (uniforms/identifications)
3. Once the fabric is made, it is __________ to make new clothes. (knitted/stitched)
4. Fibres obtained from plants and animals are called ___________ fibres. (natural/man-made)
5. Clothes made of a particular quality prevents __________ and contamination. (water/infection)

Keywords

Fibre: A long, thin, hair-like thread from which fabrics are made

Fabric: The material that is used to make clothes

Natural fibres: Fibres that are obtained from natural sources such as plants and animals

Synthetic fibres: Fibres that are not found in nature but are made by human beings

Summary

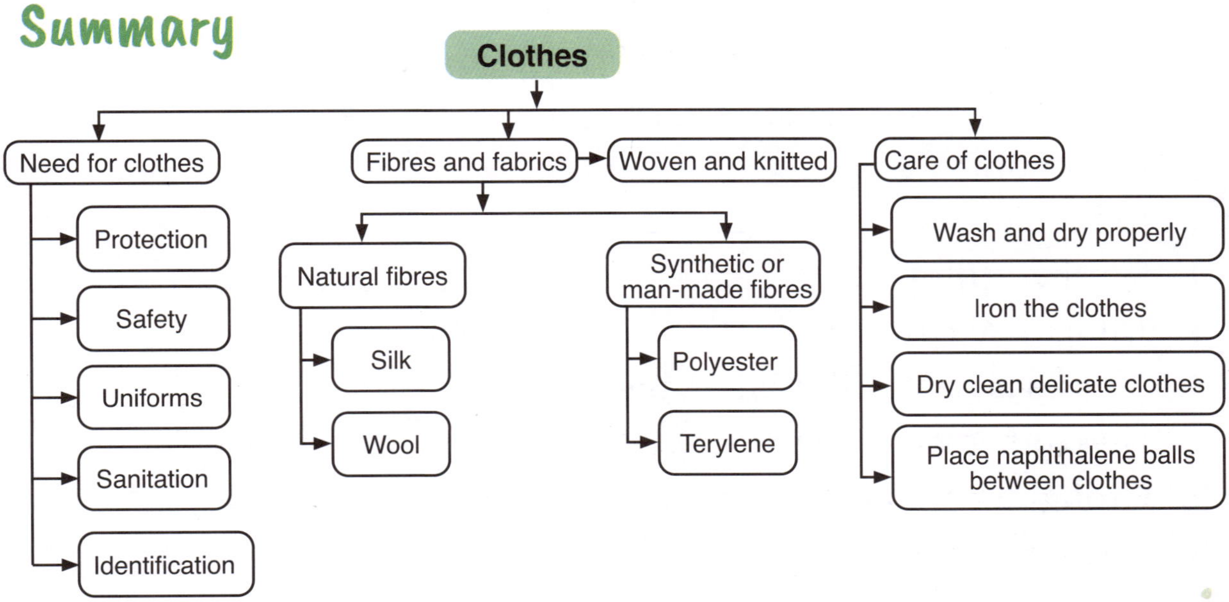

Exercise

W

A. Fill in the blanks with the correct words. ia

1. Early humans used to cover their bodies with ____________. (leaves/clothes)
2. ____________ clothes do not allow the body heat to escape. (Cotton/Woollen)
3. ____________ fibres are not found in nature. (Natural/Synthetic)
4. Linen is a ____________ fibre. (plant/animal)

B. State whether the following statements are true (T) or false (F). ia

1. Wearing clean clothes can cause diseases. ☐
2. People in Kashmir and Kerala wear the same type of clothes. ☐
3. Fabrics are made by weaving or knitting fibres together. ☐
4. Silk is made from the stem of a jute plant. ☐
5. Polyester, nylon and rayon are examples of natural fibres. ☐

C. Match the following. ia

Column A	Column B
1. Rain	(a) Protect woollen clothes
2. Cotton clothes	(b) Hair-like thread
3. Moth balls	(c) Raincoat
4. Fibre	(d) Summer

D. Give two examples for each of the following.

1. People who wear uniforms ____________
2. Plant fibres ____________
3. Animal fibres ____________
4. Synthetic fibres ____________
5. Things used to protect clothes from insects ____________

E. Give reasons for the following.

1. The clothes worn by people of Kashmir and Kerala are different.
2. Firefighters wear a specific kind of clothes.
3. Moth balls are kept between the clothes.

4. Silk clothes should not be soaked in hot water.
5. Rayon is different from cotton.

F. Answer the following questions briefly.

1. Why do we wear clothes?
2. How did early humans cover themselves?
3. What are fibres? Name the two types of fibres.
4. What is a fabric?

G. Answer the following questions.

1. What are the types of clothes we wear depending on the season?
2. Write a note on synthetic fibres.
3. Write any three ways of taking care of our clothes.

Cognitive Corner

Critical Thinking

1. Ronav helps his mother clean the dishes after dinner and gets his clothes dirty and wet in the process. What do you think might happen if he goes to bed in his dirty and wet clothes?
2. Safina wears a face mask and hand gloves while going out during the COVID-19 pandemic. Do you think it is necessary? Why or why not?

Picture Study

Unscramble the letters to identify the names of these garments.

K T E J A C

____

A N S J E

____

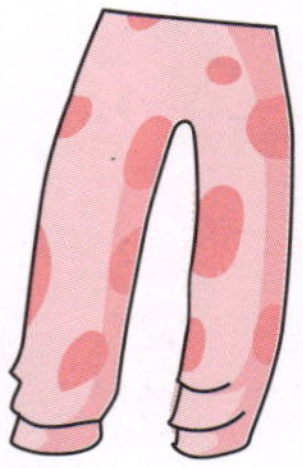

J P A M S Y A

____

A T E S R W E

____

T H S R I

____

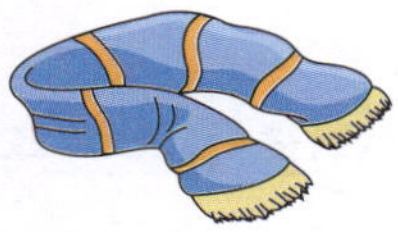

F M L E U F R

____

Project

1. Take four different types of clothes such as cotton towel, woollen sweater, nylon shirt and silk cloth. Dip them all in water. Spread them on a rope with cloth clips. Find out which one dries first. Record the timings in the table given below.

	Cotton towel	Woollen sweater	Nylon shirt	Silk cloth
Timings				

2. Prepare a note on the usage of different types of clothes. Make sentences using the words given below. An example sentence is given for you.

   Jacket, Silk, Dress, Pants, Shorts, Uniform, Skirt, Night dress, Socks

   a. Gloves: Boxers wear cushioned gloves during boxing matches.

Life Skills

Do you know how much wastes the clothes and fashion industry produce? About 31.75 kilograms of clothing is thrown away every year by a user. Think also about the pollution that will be caused by this wastage. How much do you think you have contributed to this waste? Think about it and have a discussion in your class.

Worksheet

Games and sports are an important part of our lives. There are many tournaments for cricket, football, tennis and badminton played all around the world. Sportspersons also compete in the Olympic Games in swimming, archery, weight-lifting, gymnastics and so on.

If you look at the clothes a sportsperson wears, you will see that the clothes are different for different games and sports. Sportswear is made of synthetic materials that not only looks good, but is also comfortable to wear and play in.

A. What should be the qualities of the material of a gymnast's uniform? Tick the correct options.

The clothes should be

1. comfortable.
2. stretchable.
3. stiff to touch.
4. soft to touch.

B. Do you think these clothes are made of cotton or a synthetic material?

____

C. When a football game is played, the players run a lot, sometimes in the hot sun and sometimes in the rain. So, what should be the qualities of a footballer's uniform? Tick the correct options.

The clothes should

1. be stretchable and soft.
2. irritate the skin.
3. feel comfortable when players sweat.
4. get wet easily.
5. not get wet easily and dry quickly.

D. What are the common qualities that all sportspersons have? Name any three.

____

____

____

____

9 Air, Water and Weather

Learning Checklist

- The sun and the weather
- Air
- Water

Let's Get Started

Look at the pictures given below and write the kind of weather shown in each of them.

THE SUN AND THE WEATHER

Weather is the condition of the atmosphere of a place at a particular time. It is not the same everywhere. It might be a hot and sunny day where you live, but in other parts of the world it may be cloudy or snowing. Also, it may be sunny in the morning on your way to school but it may rain in the afternoon.

The sun causes these changes in weather. The heat of the sun changes water from one form to another and also affects the movement of air. These changes in water and air bring about changes in weather.

What Causes Day and Night?

The Earth moves on its own tilted axis. This movement is called **rotation**. It takes 24 hours for the Earth to complete one rotation. At any given time, the part of the Earth that faces the sun receives light and thus has day, whereas the other part that is away from the sun does not receive light and has night. Hence, the rotation of the Earth causes day and night.

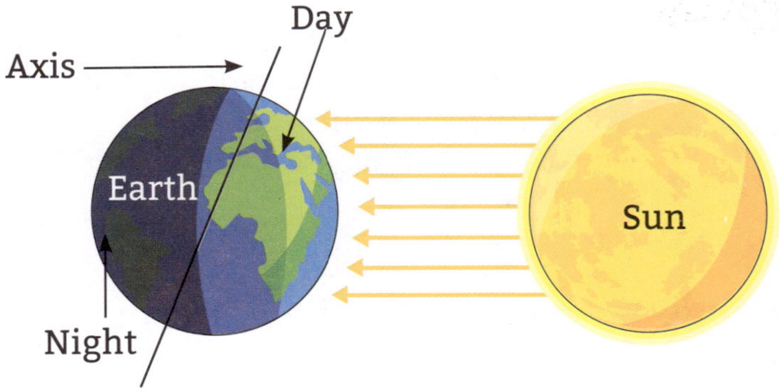

Earth's rotation causes day and night

Science in Context

The Earth spins all the time but we do not feel any of these movements. This is because the Earth moves at the same speed. We would feel the movement only if there was any change in the speed.

Why Do We Have Seasons?

The Earth moves around the sun in its own orbit. This movement is called **revolution**.

It takes 365 days and 6 hours for the Earth to complete one revolution.

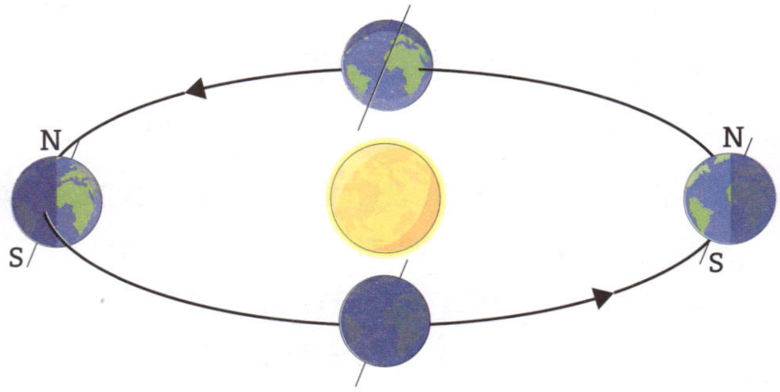

The Earth revolves around the sun

As the Earth is tilted on its axis, the portion of the Earth facing the sun has longer and warmer days. So, this portion has summer season. The portion of the Earth away from the sun has cooler and shorter days. This portion has winter season. Therefore, the revolution of the Earth causes the change in seasons.

How Do Winds Blow?

Due to the round shape of the Earth, the sun's rays do not fall evenly at all places. When a part of the Earth's surface gets heated up, the air above it becomes warm. This warm and lighter air rises up. In turn, the cool air, which is heavier, comes in to take its place. This leads to the continuous movement of air that causes winds.

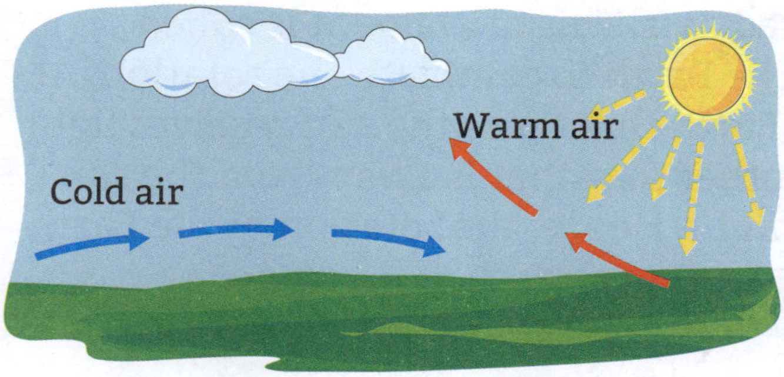

Movement of air

Try it!

How can you show that warm air rises up?

Trace a spiral on a sheet of paper. Cut out the spiral starting at the outer tip. Make a hole in the centre of the spiral and thread a string. Hold the string over a candle and see it turn!

AIR

Air is all around us. All living beings need air to breathe. Air is made up of different kinds of gases. It also contains water vapour, dust particles and smoke.

We cannot see air but we can feel air when it blows. Moving air is called **wind**. A gentle wind is called **breeze** whereas a strong wind is called **gale**. Very fast and strong winds are called **storms**.

If we go to a seashore on a hot and sunny day, we will find the sand on the shore very hot and the seawater cool. This happens because land gets heated up faster than water. It also cools down faster than water. This difference gives rise to sea breeze and land breeze. Let us learn how.

Sea Breeze and Land Breeze

During the day, land gets heated up much faster than the water in the sea. As the land becomes hot, it heats the air above it. This hot air rises up and the cool air from the sea blows towards the land to take its place. This wind that blows from the sea towards the land during the day is called the **sea breeze**.

At night, land cools down much faster than the sea. As a result, the air above the land also cools down. The air above the sea is still warmer. This warm air rises up and the cool air from the land rushes towards the sea to take its place. This wind that blows from the land towards the sea at night is called the **land breeze**.

Thus, we feel the sea breeze during daytime and the land breeze during night.

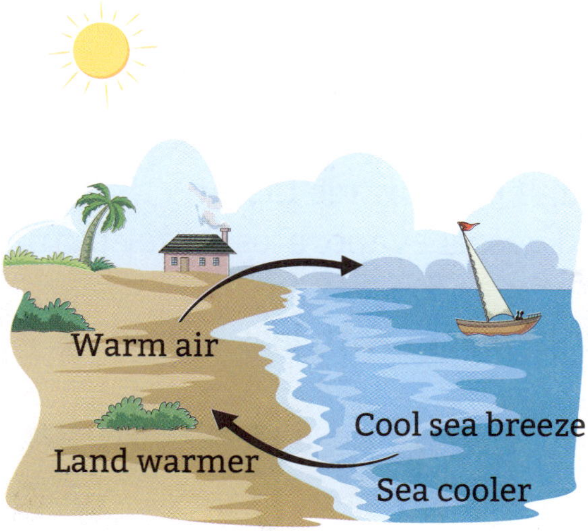

Day

Night

Revise and Recall

Fill in the blanks with the correct words.

1. The ____________ causes changes in weather. (sun/moon)
2. The ____________ of the Earth causes day and night. (revolution/rotation)
3. Land gets heated up ____________ than the sea. (faster/slower)
4. We feel ____________ breeze during daytime. (land/sea)

WATER

Water is one of the basic necessities of life. Nearly three-fourths of the Earth's surface is covered with water. Human beings, plants and animals—all need water to live.

Water exists in three different forms—ice, water and water vapour. Water changes from one form to another on heating or cooling.

Evaporation

The process in which water changes into water vapour on heating is called **evaporation**. We have learned that water is also present in the atmosphere in the form of water vapour. The amount of water vapour present in the atmosphere is known as **humidity**. When the weather is very hot, more water gets evaporated, which makes the weather humid. Thus, we can say that the sun is responsible for the change of water into water vapour.

The rate of evaporation depends on the following factors:

- **Wind speed:** A bowl of water kept under a fan evaporates faster.
- **Heat:** When a pot of water is heated, it evaporates faster.
- **Surface area:** Water kept in a broad vessel evaporates faster than the water in a narrow vessel.
- **Humidity:** Water evaporates faster in places with less humidity.

Condensation

Condensation

Water drops on leaves

The process in which water vapour changes into water on cooling is called **condensation**. For example, when a cold lid is placed on a pot with boiling water, we can see water drops on the underside of the lid after sometime. This is because condensation takes place when the water vapour touches the cold surface of the lid. Hence, it cools down and forms water droplets. Clouds are formed by the process of condensation. During winter, early in the morning we can see tiny droplets of water on grass and leaves. These tiny droplets are called **dew**. They are formed by the condensation of water vapour present in the air.

Activity 1

Aim: To observe evaporation and condensation

Materials required: Cotton handkerchief, a glass of water and ice cubes

Procedure:

1. Wet the handkerchief and spread it out in the sun to dry.
2. Observe it after an hour or two. What do you notice?
3. Now, fill the glass with water and put some ice cubes in it.
4. Observe it after some time. What do you see?

Observation: The handkerchief dries after some time. Small droplets of water can be seen on the outer surface of the glass.

Conclusion: Water from the handkerchief evaporated as water vapour, that is why it dried. Water vapour from the air condensed on the outer surface of the glass, that is why the small water droplets can be seen.

Water Cycle

The sun heats the water in seas, rivers, lakes and ponds, and changes it into water vapour. This water vapour rises up in the atmosphere where it condenses and changes into tiny droplets of water. These water droplets join together to form clouds. Inside the clouds, the tiny water droplets join to form bigger drops. When these drops become heavy, they fall on the Earth's surface as rain. This process forms a continuous cycle in nature known as the **water cycle**.

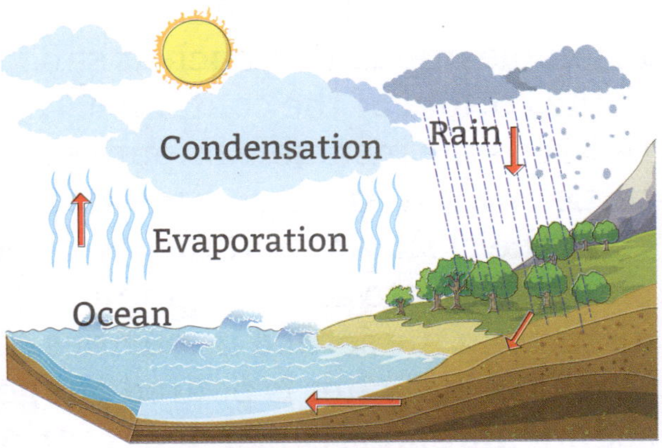

The water cycle

Science in Context

When water vapour condenses on dust particles in the air in the early mornings, mist is formed. When dense clouds are formed closer to the ground, fog occurs. These are forms of condensation.

Science in Context

The condensation of atmospheric water vapour on the Earth's surface is called **precipitation**. The main forms of precipitation include rain, sleet, hail and snow.

Water Purification

Water may contain substances such as sand, dirt and germs, which make the water unfit for use. Drinking impure water may cause diseases. So, water should be purified before using it for drinking and cooking.

Let us learn about some methods by which we can purify water.

Boiling

One of the easiest methods to purify water is to boil it for 10 minutes. Boiling kills most of the germs present in the water. Boiled water should be cooled and then stored in a clean and covered container.

Sedimentation and Decantation

In this method, water is allowed to stand undisturbed in a container for some time. Insoluble impurities, such as sand, settle at the bottom of the container. The process in which the insoluble impure substances settle down is called **sedimentation**. Then the clear water at the top is slowly poured out into another container without disturbing the settled impurities. The process in which the water is poured out gently after sedimentation is called **decantation**.

Sedimentation Decantation

Filtration

The process of separating insoluble impurities from a liquid using a filter paper is known as **filtration**. In this process, water is passed through a filter paper kept in a funnel. The impurities are left behind on the filter paper, and only pure water passes through it and gets collected in the container.

Filtration

Water taps usually have filters to purify water.

Chlorination

Addition of chlorine (a chemical) to kill the germs present in water is called **chlorination**.

Save Water

> **Word Web**
>
> [1]**Scarce**: less; not available in plenty

Water is a valuable natural resource. We need water for our daily activities such as drinking, cooking, bathing and growing plants.

We should not waste water because it is precious and scarce[1]. There are places where people walk miles to get only a pot of clean drinking water.

Following are some of the ways to save water.

- Do not leave the tap open while brushing your teeth.
- Turn off the tap properly so that no water drips. Dripping leads to the wastage of water.
- Use only a bucket of water to take bath.
- Use a watering can to water the plants.
- Wash your car using water in a bucket instead of using a hosepipe.

Keywords

Rotation: The movement of the Earth on its tilted axis

Revolution: The movement of the Earth in its orbit around the sun

Sea breeze: The cool air that blows from the sea towards the land during daytime

Land breeze: The cool air that blows from land towards the sea at night

Sedimentation: The process in which the insoluble impurities settle down at the bottom of liquid in a container

Decantation: The process in which the clean water is poured out gently after sedimentation

Filtration: The process of separating insoluble impurities from a liquid using a filter paper

Chlorination: The process of adding chlorine to water to kill germs

Summary

Air, Water and Weather

- **Air**
  - Wind: Moving air
  - Breeze: Gentle wind
    - Sea breeze
      - Sea to land during day
    - Land breeze
      - Land to sea during night
  - Gale: Strong wind
  - Storm: Very fast and strong wind
- **Water**
  - Evaporation
    - Wind speed
    - Heat
    - Surface area
    - Humidity
  - Condensation
    - Dew
  - Water cycle
    - Evaporation of ocean water
    - Condensation to form clouds
    - Precipitates as rain
  - Water purification
    - Boiling
    - Sedimentation and decantation
    - Filtration
    - Chlorination
  - Save water
- **Weather**
  - Sun
    - Causes the change in weather
  - Day and night
    - Rotation of the Earth
  - Seasons
    - Revolution of the Earth
  - Wind blows
    - Warm air moves up
    - Cool air moves down

Decantation

Sedimentation

Evaporation Condensation

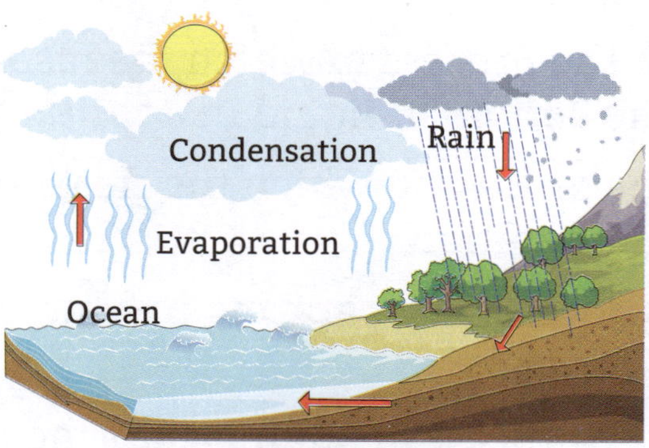

The water cycle

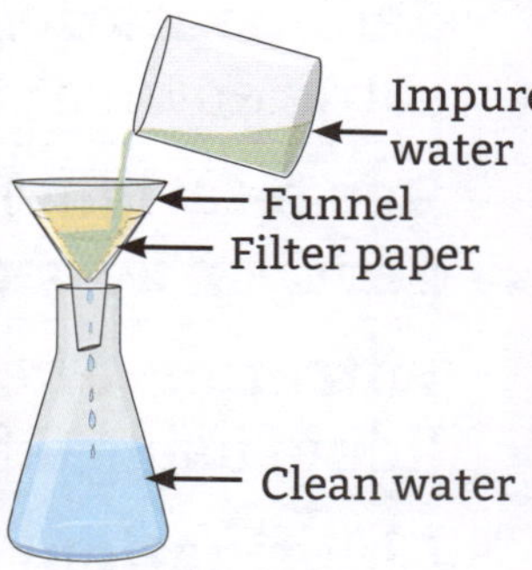

Filtration

Exercise

w

A. Choose the correct option for each of the following.

ia

1. Day and night are caused due to the
   (a) Rotation of the sun (b) Rotation of the Earth
   (c) Revolution of the sun (d) Revolution of the Earth
2. How long does it take for the Earth to complete one revolution?
   (a) 24 hours (b) 365 days and 6 hours
   (c) 365 days (d) 366 days
3. The process in which water vapour changes into water on cooling is known as
   (a) Evaporation (b) Condensation (c) Melting (d) Freezing
4. Water changes into water vapour by the process of
   (a) Condensation (b) Sea breeze
   (c) Evaporation (d) Land breeze
5. Which of the following processes cannot be used to purify water with insoluble impurities?
   (a) Sedimentation (b) Filtration
   (c) Decantation (d) Boiling

B. Fill in the blanks with the correct words.

ia

1. The movement of the Earth around the sun in its own orbit is known as ________. (rotation/revolution)
2. Land gets heated up ________ than water. (faster/slower)
3. Movement of cool air from land towards the sea is known as ________ breeze. (land/sea)
4. Moving air is called ________. (clouds/wind)
5. The process in which the insoluble impurities settle down at the bottom of a liquid is known as ________. (sedimentation/decantation)

C. State whether the following statements are true (T) or false (F).

ia

1. Different places have different weather conditions for a given period of time. ☐
2. The rotation of the Earth causes the change in seasons. ☐

3. Air contains water vapour, dust particles and smoke. ☐
4. Humidity is the amount of water vapour present in the atmosphere. ☐
5. One of the easiest methods to purify water is filtration. ☐

D. Give one word for each of the following. ia

1. The movement of the Earth on its own tilted axis ________
2. The cool air that blows from the land towards the sea at night ________
3. Very fast and strong wind ________
4. The process of adding chlorine to water to kill germs ________
5. The process in which water is poured out gently after sedimentation ________

E. Give reasons for the following.

1. On a hot sunny day on a sea shore, the sand on the shore will be very hot and the seawater will be cool.
2. Water kept in a broad vessel evaporates faster than the water kept in a narrow vessel.
3. During winter mornings, we can see dew on grass and leaves.
4. Water should be purified before using it for drinking and cooking.
5. It is advised to use a watering can to water plants.

F. Answer the following questions briefly.

1. Define weather.
2. What is humidity?
3. What is evaporation?
4. Give two examples of condensation that you come across in your daily life.
5. Why should we purify water before drinking?

G. Answer the following questions.

1. What causes winds to blow? Explain with a diagram.
2. Describe the formation of sea breeze and land breeze.
3. Describe the factors that affect the rate of evaporation.
4. Describe any two processes that can be used to purify water.
5. Why should we save water? Write any three ways to save water.

Cognitive Corner

Critical Thinking

1. Rahul was feeling very thirsty after playing out in the sun. He took out a bottle of cold water from the refrigerator. After some time, he saw tiny droplets of water on the outer surface of the bottle. Can you explain why this happened?
2. Cloudy days are warmer. Why?
3. Are wind and humidity related to temperature of a place? How?

Picture Study

Label the given picture and write the name of the process shown here.

Name of the process: ______________

Project

Newspapers give daily weather forecasts. With the help of an elder, collect newspaper cuttings of weather forecasts for a week. Paste these in your scrapbook. Is the forecast the same for all days?

Life Skills

We know that the one of the most valuable natural resources in our world today is water. It is essential for us to keep it clean, safe and fresh. However, there is a scarcity of good quality drinking water for most of the people around the world. If we continue to waste and pollute water, this will become one of the most serious challenges to all of us in the future. It is your right to have access to clean water, but your responsibility is not to waste or pollute water.

Become a 'Wise Water Hero' by listing and practicing the water conservation methods you can follow in schools, home and playgrounds.

6 CLEAN WATER AND SANITATION

Worksheet

Many places in the world do not get enough clean water. It is due to the improper sanitation. Sanitation is the process of keeping places clean and healthy, especially by providing a sewage system and clean water supply. Many activities that we do also lead to improper sanitation and hence shortage of clean water.

Observe the pictures given below. These are some of the problems that lead to the shortage of clean water. How can you solve these problems? Draw a poster showing the solution beside each picture. Also, write a slogan for your posters.

10 The Solar System

Learning Checklist

- The solar system
- Satellites
- Stars
- Movements of the Earth

Let's Get Started

Look at the pictures given below and answer the questions.

What are the pits on the moon's surface called?

____

What is the name of this constellation of stars?

____

When we look at the night sky, we see the moon, planets and stars. Stars twinkle in the night sky but planets do not. In the daytime, we see the sun in the sky.

In this chapter, let us learn more about the sun, moon, stars and planets.

SOLAR SYSTEM

a

The sun, the eight planets, their moons and the dwarf planets together form the **solar system**. The planets revolve around the sun in their fixed paths called **orbits**. The eight planets (nearest to farthest from the sun) are Mercury, Venus, Earth, Mars, Jupiter, Saturn, Uranus and Neptune.

Sun

The sun is at the centre of the solar system. It is a huge ball of hot gases that continuously gives out heat and light.

Science in Context

The average distance of the sun from the Earth is about 150 million kilometres. This distance is called one astronomical unit (1 AU). Astronomical unit is used for measuring the distance of planets and satellites within the solar system.

Mercury

Mercury is the planet nearest to the sun. It is the smallest planet in the solar system. It does not have any moon.

Venus

Venus is the second planet from the sun. It is the hottest planet in the solar system. Venus is also called the morning star or evening star as it can be seen in the sky at dawn or dusk. Venus does not have any moon.

Earth

Earth is the third planet from the sun. Most of its surface is covered with water. It is the only planet where life is known to exist. It has one moon revolving around it. Earth is surrounded by a blanket of air called the **atmosphere** that protects us from the harmful radiations from the sun.

Mars

Mars is the fourth planet from the sun. It is the second smallest planet in the solar system and is about half the size of the Earth. Mars is also called the red planet because the soil and rocks on its surface are red in colour. Mars has two moons.

Wonder!

The highest mountain in the solar system, called **Olympus Mons** (Mount Olympus), is on the surface of Mars. It is about three times taller than Mount Everest. The two moons of Mars are called Phobos and Deimos.

Science in Context

Mangalyaan is India's Mars orbiter mission, which was successfully launched on 5 November 2013 by the Indian Space Research Organization (ISRO). It was launched from the Satish Dhawan Space Centre, Sriharikota, Andhra Pradesh.

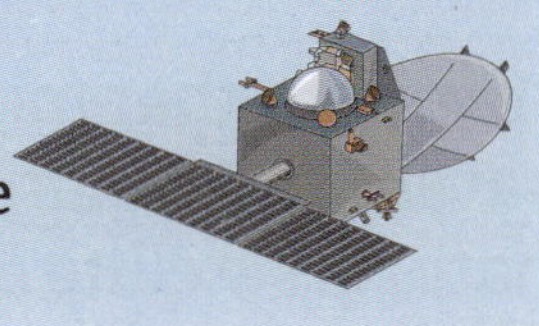

Jupiter

Jupiter is the fifth planet from the sun and the largest planet in the solar system. Jupiter is also the fastest spinning planet. Because of its fast spin, the planet pulls the clouds surrounding it. This results in the formation of a striped pattern on it. Jupiter has 95 known moons revolving around it.

Saturn

Saturn is the sixth planet from the sun. It is the second largest planet in the solar system. Saturn has a prominent ring system around it. It has 146 known moons revolving around it.

Uranus

Uranus is the seventh planet from the sun. It is the third largest planet in the solar system. Uranus has about 27 known moons.

Neptune

Neptune is the eighth and the farthest planet from the sun. It is the fourth largest planet in the solar system. Neptune has around 14 known moons.

Dwarf Planets

A dwarf planet is an object that revolves around the sun but does not belong to the category of planets.

In 2006, the International Astronomical Union (IAU) classified Pluto as a dwarf planet, though it was considered as a planet until 2006. Ceres, Makemake, Eris, etc. are some other dwarf planets in our solar system.

SATELLITES

An object that moves around a planet in an orbit is called its **moon** or **satellite**. All planets except Mercury and Venus have moons. Moon is the natural satellite of the Earth.

Natural Satellite: Moon

Moon is about 3,84,400 km away from the Earth. It completes one revolution around the Earth in 27 days. It does not have its own light but appears bright as it reflects the light of the sun. Moon does not have an atmosphere, unlike the Earth, to protect itself from very hot or cold conditions.

The moon

So, the temperature on the moon can rise upto 117 °C at noon and come down to –173 °C at night. The surface of the moon is covered with large pits or holes called **craters**.

Artificial Satellites

The Earth has a lot of man-made satellites revolving around it. These are called artificial satellites and revolve around the Earth in fixed orbits. One of the first artificial satellites to be sent into space was SPUTNIK-1. The first artificial satellite to be sent into space by India was called Aryabhatta. It was launched on 19 March 1975.

Revise and Recall

Name the following.

1. The nearest planet to the sun ____________________
2. The hottest planet in the solar system ____________________
3. The planet that appears red in colour ____________________
4. The largest planet in the solar system ____________________
5. A dwarf planet ____________________

STARS

Stars are huge balls of hot gases that give out heat and light continuously. They appear as tiny points in the sky because they are very far away from the Earth.

The sun is also a star. It is the nearest star to our planet, which is why it appears big and bright.

Why do we not see any stars in the sky during daytime? This is because the sun is very near to the Earth and hence looks much brighter as compared to the other stars that are far away. Hence, we cannot see other stars or the moon during daytime.

MOVEMENTS OF THE EARTH

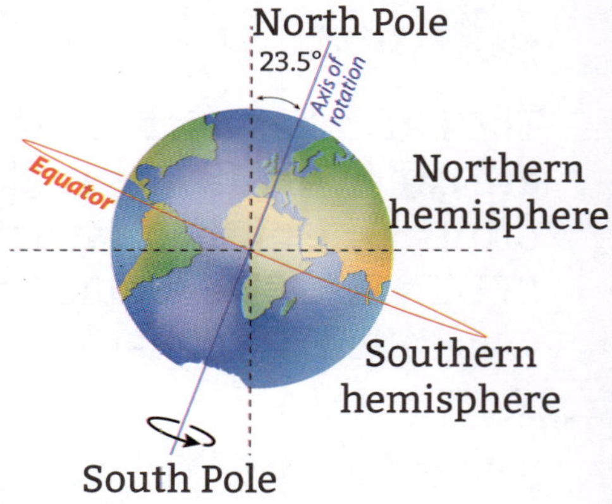

As the Earth revolves around the sun, it also rotates on its own axis. The **axis of the Earth** is an imaginary line passing through the North Pole, the South Pole and the centre of the Earth. This axis of rotation is tilted at an angle of about 23.5°. Another imaginary line on the surface of the Earth is called the **equator**. It is at equal distance from the North Pole and the South Pole. The equator divides the Earth into two equal halves called the northern hemisphere and the southern hemisphere.

How Are Days and Nights Formed?

The Earth completes one rotation on its own axis in about 24 hours, that is, one day. Day and night are caused by the rotation of the Earth. Only half of the Earth faces the sun at a time. Thus, the countries on this half have daytime. The other half that faces away from the sun at this time has night. As the Earth rotates, the places that had night eventually come to face the sun and experience day, and the places that had day experience night.

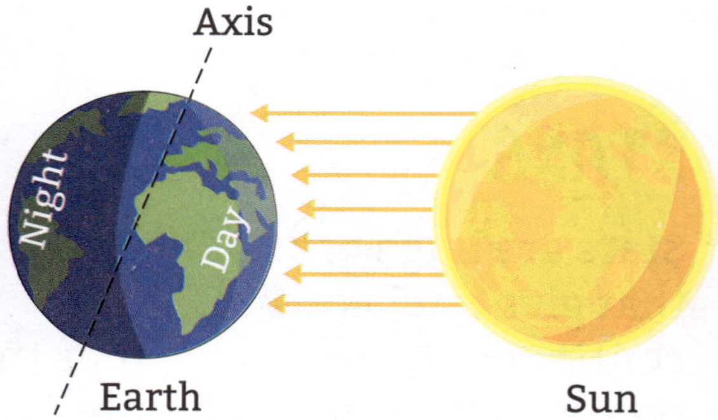

How Are Seasons Formed?

The Earth completes one revolution around the sun in about one year. The revolution of the Earth and the tilt of its axis together cause seasons on the Earth. Because of the tilt of the Earth's axis, the sun's rays fall directly on either the northern or the southern hemisphere. The part of the Earth that receives more sunlight will have summer and the other half will have winter.

As the Earth moves around the sun, after about six months, the part that had summer will now have winter and the part that had winter will now have summer. Therefore, when countries in the northern hemisphere have summer, countries in the southern hemisphere have winter.

For example, when we have summer in India, which is in the northern hemisphere, Australia, in the southern hemisphere, has winter.

Apart from the summer and winter seasons, India has two more seasons called autumn and spring. Autumn comes after summer and before winter, while spring comes after winter and before summer. It is neither very hot nor very cold during these seasons; these seasons are pleasant.

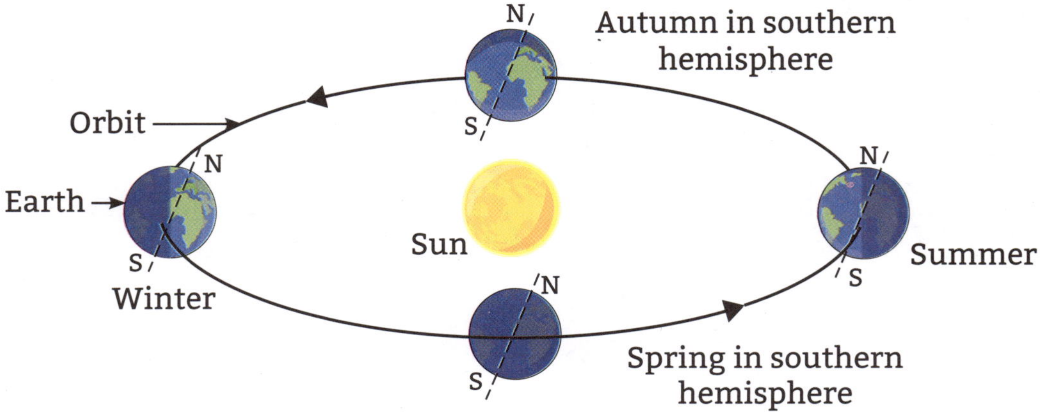

Earth's revolution around the sun

Revise and Recall

Fill in the blanks with the correct words.

1. The sun is a ______________. (planet/star)
2. ___________ is the natural satellite of the Earth. (Moon/Mars)
3. An object that moves around a planet in an orbit is called its ____________. (satellite/star)
4. A _________ is a natural object that revolves around the sun but does not belong to the category of planets. (satellite/dwarf planet)
5. Seasons are formed because of the Earth's ______________. (revolution/rotation)
6. Pluto is now considered to be a ________. (planet/dwarf planet)
7. The pits on the surface of the moon are called ________. (craters/valleys)
8. The angle of tilt of the Earth's axis is ___________. (23.5°/45.5°)
9. The Earth completes one rotation in _________. (a day/an hour)
10. It takes about _______ months to change the season from summer to winter in a particular region on the Earth. (six/three)

Keywords

Planet: Objects in the solar system that revolve around the sun

Satellite: Objects in the solar system that revolve around the planets

Orbit: The fixed path along which the planets move around the sun

Axis: An imaginary line passing through the North Pole, the South Pole and the centre of the Earth

Equator: An imaginary line on the Earth's surface that divides it into two equal halves: the northern hemisphere and the southern hemisphere

Summary

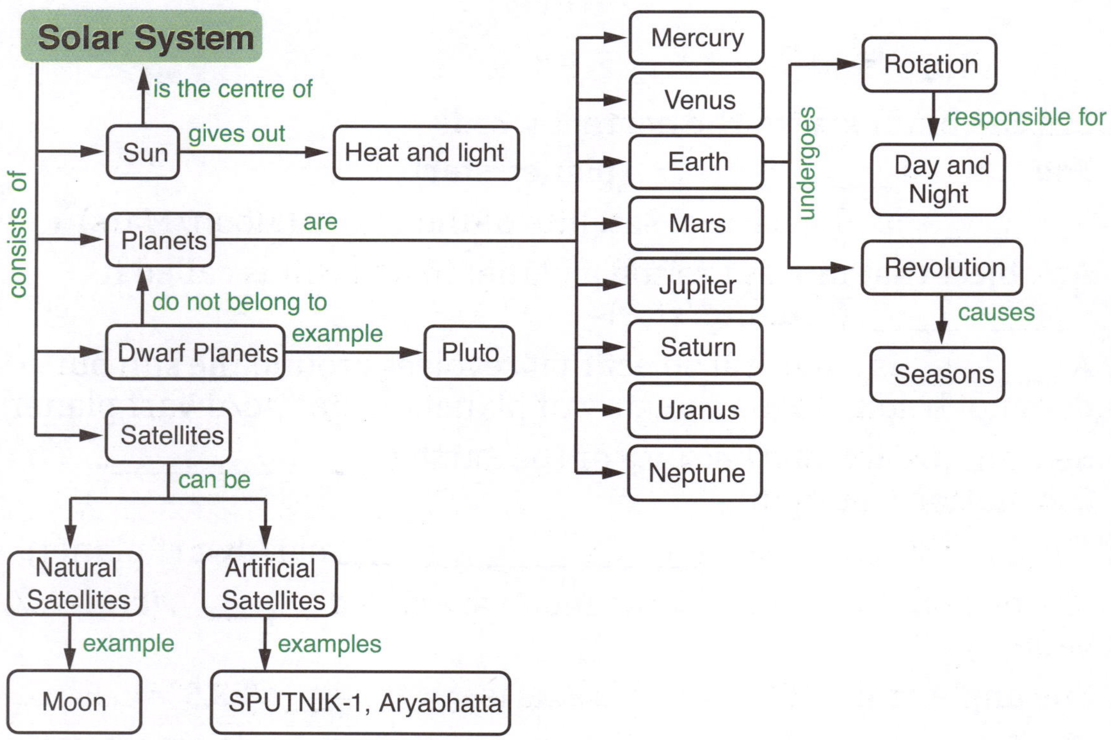

Exercise

W

A. Choose the correct option for each of the following. ia

1. The sun is a
   (a) Planet (b) Satellite
   (c) Star (d) Dwarf planet
2. The nearest planet to the sun is
   (a) Venus (b) Mercury (c) Neptune (d) Mars
3. The biggest planet in the solar system is
   (a) Mars (b) Jupiter (c) Saturn (d) Pluto
4. The planet that has a prominent ring system around it is
   (a) Mars (b) Jupiter (c) Saturn (d) Uranus
5. Which among the following is a satellite?
   (a) Sun (b) Mercury (c) Moon (d) Pluto

B. State whether the following statements are true (T) or false (F). ia

1. Mars is called a red planet. ☐
2. Moon is the artificial satellite of the Earth. ☐
3. Uranus is the farthest planet from the sun. ☐
4. Neptune is a dwarf planet. ☐
5. Saturn is the second-largest planet of the solar system. ☐

C. Give one word for each of the following. ia

1. The smallest planet in the solar system ____________
2. The planet on which life exists ____________
3. The natural satellite of the Earth ____________
4. The first artificial satellite sent into space by India ____________
5. An imaginary line that divides the Earth into two equal halves ____________

D. Give reasons for the following.

1. Venus is also called the morning star or evening star.
2. The atmosphere acts like a blanket around the Earth.
3. Life is not possible on the Earth's moon.
4. Mars is also called the red planet.
5. We do not see any stars in the sky during daytime

E. Answer the following questions briefly.

1. What is the solar system?
2. Name any two dwarf planets of the solar system.
3. What is a satellite?
4. Why does Jupiter have a striped pattern?
5. What are the two factors that cause seasons on the Earth?

F. Answer the following questions.

1. Briefly describe any three objects of the solar system.
2. What is the difference between natural and artificial satellites?
3. Write a note on stars.
4. How are days and nights caused? Explain with a diagram.

Cognitive Corner

Critical Thinking

1. Our planet Earth is considered to be a unique planet. Why?
2. What are the essential things astronauts need to survive in a satellite in space?
3. When is National Moon day? Write its importance.

Picture Study

Look at the picture given below and label the equator, the axis, the North Pole and the South Pole.

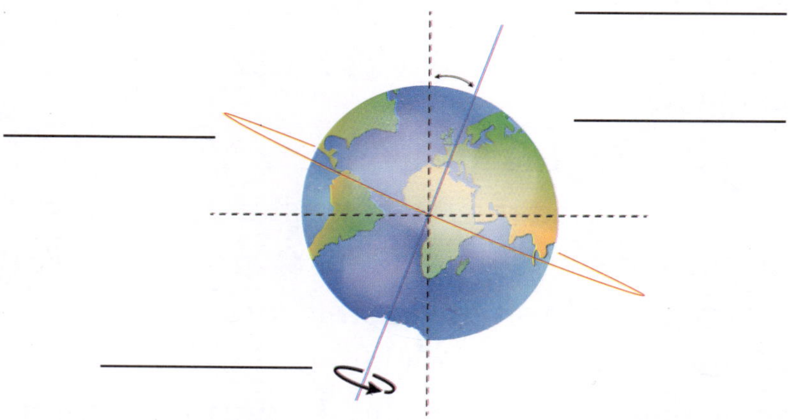

Project

1. Make a solar system model using balls.

Materials required: Nine plastic balls of different sizes, eight narrow sticks of different lengths, paints of different colours.

Procedure:

a. Take nine balls of different sizes.

b. Use the biggest ball as the sun and paint it in yellow colour. Use the smaller balls as Mercury, Venus, Earth and Mars, and bigger balls for Jupiter, Saturn, Uranus and Neptune.

c. Paint Mercury and Venus in light orange colour and the Earth in pale blue colour. Use red colour to paint Mars. Colour Jupiter and Saturn in brown. Colour Uranus and Neptune in deep blue.

d. Fix each of these balls (planets) at the ends of the sticks by piercing the stick into each ball. Use the shortest stick for mercury and longest stick for Neptune. Draw a circle on the biggest ball used as Sun and fix the other ends of the sticks on this ball (sun) along the circle drawn at equal distances.

e. Make a small ring using a thick paper sheet or a thin sponge sheet and fix it on the ball selected for Saturn.

f. Now, make a circular stand using thermocol and fix the sun (ball) on it. Your model of solar system is ready.

2. India has a wealthy tradition in astronomy from ancient times. Find out the contributions of great astronomers in India, starting from Aryabhata and Varahamihira to the modern astronomers such as Subramanyam Chandrasekhar. Make a presentation based on your findings.

Life Skills

Conduct a research on the following topics and collect the pictures and information related to it. Prepare a space magazine including pictures, news, notes etc. of artificial satellites and astronauts.

- "India's satellite launching vehicles"
- "India's pride – Chandrayaan, Chandrayan I and Chandrayan II"
- "India's Mission to mars – Mangalyaan"

Worksheet

Man has always been fascinated by space and longed to know what lay beyond the Earth's boundary. Voyager 1 and Voyager 2 are two spacecrafts which were launched by NASA in 1977 from Florida, USA. The main aim of sending these probes into space was to conduct close-up studies of Jupiter and Saturn.

Each space probe carried a golden record which had a collection of sights, sounds and greetings from the Earth. These included 117 images, greetings in 54 languages, sounds of storms, volcanoes, rocket launches, aircrafts and animals. This was done in case it met life in outer space.

Draw a picture you would like to send into space to show what it is like to be on the Earth.

11 Keeping the Earth Green

Learning Checklist

- Importance of trees
- Deforestation
- Saving trees

Let's Get Started

Look at the two pictures given below. Identify the words that describe these pictures and write in the space given below.

Trees　Lake　Tree stumps　Rocks　Dry soil　Green grass

___________________________ ___________________________

___________________________ ___________________________

___________________________ ___________________________

___________________________ ___________________________

Plants make our surroundings look green and beautiful. Plants are of great use and importance to us.

Over the years, there has been an increase in the human population. To meet their needs, human beings have destroyed forests by cutting down trees without planting more of them.

In this chapter, let us learn about the importance of trees, the ill-effects of destroying forests and the ways to save trees.

IMPORTANCE OF TREES

Trees are very important to us. They provide us with many things that are necessary in our day-to-day life. Some of them are as follows:

- Trees give us food in the form of fruits, vegetables, spices, seeds, etc.
- They provide us clean air to breathe.
- Trees help in the formation of rain.
- They keep our surroundings cool.
- The roots of trees hold the soil and prevent soil erosion.
- Trees give us wood to make paper, timber to make furniture, windows and doors, firewood for fuel, etc.

Forest

Timber

Furniture

Firewood

- We also use herbs and other plants of medicinal value to make medicines.

Science in Context

The rubber used in making erasers, tyres, rubber balls and shoes is made from latex of rubber trees. Latex is a white, milk-like liquid produced by these trees, which is collected and processed further to form rubber.

DEFORESTATION

Destroying forests by cutting down a large number of trees is called **deforestation**. Deforestation has many harmful effects on the environment such as less rainfall, impure air and soil erosion. Deforestation also leads to shortage of food and shelter for wild animals.

Cutting trees

Deforestation

The harmful effects of deforestation can be reduced by planting more trees than what we cut down.

SAVING TREES

Saving the trees

Following are some ways to save trees and keep our Earth green:

- We should plant more trees than we cut down. Planting trees in large numbers is called **afforestation**.
- We should not waste products such as paper that we get from trees. Such products should be used wisely and, if possible, reused.
- We should not use trees for firewood.
- We should take steps to control and prevent forest fires caused during the summer months.

In India, we have a tree-planting festival called *Vana Mahotsava*, which is celebrated every year in July. In this festival, people plant trees in homes, school, offices, parks, etc.

The World Environment Day is celebrated each year on 5 June to create awareness on taking steps to protect the environment. People are encouraged to plant more trees all over the world.

Children planting a tree

Revise and Recall

Fill in the blanks with the correct words.

1. ______________ trees in large numbers is called afforestation. (Planting/Destroying)
2. Forest fires are caused during the ______________ months. (winter/summer)
3. The World Environment Day is celebrated each year on __________ (5 June/15 August)
4. In India, we have a tree-planting festival called ______________, which is celebrated every year in July. (*Vana Mahotsava*/World Environment day)

Keywords

Deforestation: Destroying forests by cutting down a large number of trees

Afforestation: Planting trees in large numbers

Summary

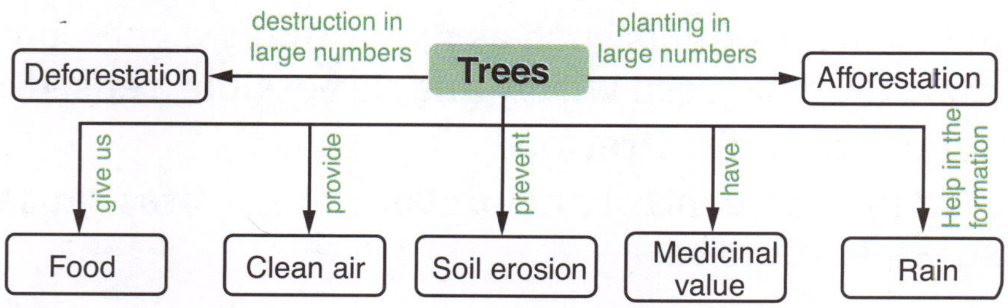

Exercise

W

A. Choose the correct option for each of the following. ia

1. Trees make our surroundings clean and ____________.
   (a) Green (b) Blue (c) Grey (d) White
2. Which of the following is not obtained from trees?
   (a) Timber (b) Firewood (c) Medicines (d) Plastic
3. Roots of trees hold the soil and prevent
   (a) Afforestation (b) Deforestation
   (c) Soil erosion (d) None of these
4. Which of the following is not an effect of deforestation?
   (a) Air becomes impure (b) Less rainfall
   (c) Soil conservation (d) All of these

B. State whether the following statements are true (T) or false (F) ia

1. Only people in the villages use trees. ☐
2. Trees are home for many animals. ☐
3. Trees help in the formation of rain. ☐
4. We should not waste paper. ☐
5. *Vana Mahotsava* is celebrated in December. ☐

C. Write one word for each of the following. ia

1. Trees hold this to prevent erosion ____________
2. Cutting down trees in large numbers ____________
3. Planting trees in large numbers ____________
4. Trees give us this to make furniture ____________

D. Give reasons for the following.

1. Plants are of great use and importance to us.
2. Destroying forests has many harmful effects on the environment.
3. A walk in the park among trees energizes us.
4. The roots of trees prevent soil erosion.
5. We should we use paper wisely.

E. Answer the following questions briefly.

1. Name any four things that we get from trees.
2. How can the harmful effects of deforestation be reduced?
3. When is the World Environment Day celebrated?
4. What is *Vana Mahotsava*?

F. Answer the following questions.

1. Explain the importance of trees.
2. Explain deforestation and its harmful effects.
3. Describe the ways to save trees.

Cognitive Corner

Critical Thinking

1. We regularly use some products in school that we get from trees. Can you name these products?
2. Awungshi lives in a house with no plants in her surroundings. She often describes her house as hot. What can make her house cool?

Picture Study

Look at the picture and write a few lines about the picture.

____

____

____

____

Project

1. Make a poster on the measures we can take to keep our Earth green. You can draw or paste related pictures to make the poster colourful.
2. Slogans such as 'Each one plant one' encourage people to plant trees. Make some slogans of your own on the need to plant trees and save the environment. Write them on a chart paper and display it in your school.

Life Skills

Paper is obtained from trees. Trees are made into a pulp to make paper. Therefore, wastage of paper leads to destruction of more trees.

What can you do to reduce wastage of paper and hence destruction of trees? Write any five steps that you can follow.

Worksheet

The Earth is becoming warmer. As a result, the polar ice caps and glaciers across the world are melting. Forests are becoming drier and incidents of forest fires are increasing. We have now become aware that planting trees on a large scale is one of the ways that will help the Earth recover.

The Indian government has been organizing programmes such as *Vana Mahotsava*. Many leaders and communities have joined hands to plant trees after any man-made or natural destruction of vegetation.

A. Have you ever participated in *Vana Mahotsava* or some programme like this? If yes, write down your experience in 4–5 sentences.

B. Suppose your class is organizing *Vana Mahotsava* in your school. Create stickers that can be distributed to everyone. Make it interesting to get the attention of everyone and they would participate happily. Draw your designs in the circles provided below.

12 Soil

Learning Checklist

- Formation of soil
- Soil composition
- Soil profile
- Soil erosion
- Soil conservation

Let's Get Started

Find the words given in the box from the wordsearch. Words may read forward or backwards. One has been done for you.

Air Sand Rocks Clay Water Earthworm

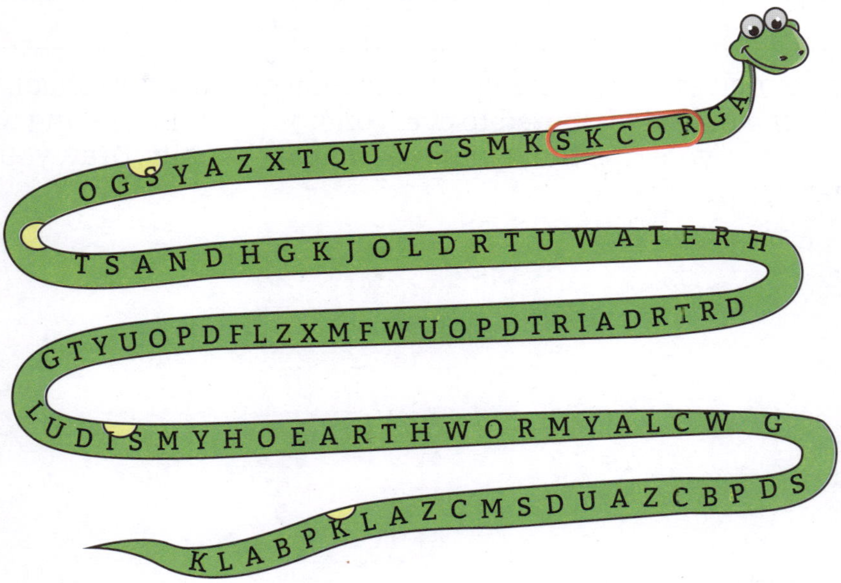

In addition to air and water, soil is also essential for life on the Earth. Plants grow in the soil and we know that all living beings depend on plants for survival. Soil is also home to many insects and animals. Let us learn more about the formation and properties of soil in this chapter.

FORMATION OF SOIL

Weathering of rocks

Formation of soil is a slow process. It takes thousands of years to form just 1 cm of soil. Big rocks are broken down into smaller pieces due to the heat of the sun, strong winds and flowing water. The rocks get heated up due to the sun's rays and expand during the day. They contract at night when they cool down. This continuous process forms cracks in rocks which are further broken down by wind and flowing water. Roots of plants and burrowing animals can also break rocks. When the roots grow, they may enter into the rocks and break them into smaller pieces.

The natural breakdown of rocks is known as **weathering**.

Different colours of soil

The smaller rocks are further broken down into fine particles. With time, the continuous weathering of rocks creates a thin layer of soil. Remains of dead plants and animals (called **humus**) mix with soil and make it fertile. The colour of soil varies from place to place. Soil can be black, dark brown or red in colour.

Thus, soil can be defined as the topmost layer of the Earth's surface, which consists of sand, remains of dead plants and animals, minerals and some amount of air and water.

SOIL COMPOSITION

Soil is made up of many things. The five basic components of soil are given below:

- Rock material
- Organic material
- Air
- Water
- Soil creatures

Go Green

Kitchen wastes can enrich your garden soil with humus.

Rock material: Substances such as sand, silt and clay are formed due to the weathering of rocks. These form the inorganic components of soil. Sand and silt are small particles of rock. Pebbles are the larger components of soil. Clay is composed of very fine particles that are closely packed.

Organic material: Organic material consists of **humus**. It is the dark brown substance formed due to the decay of dead plants and animals. Humus provides nutrients to the plants for their growth and helps the soil to hold more water.

Science in Context

Air found in soil is rich in carbon dioxide and poor in oxygen. This is because most of the oxygen is used by soil organisms for breathing.

Air: Soil also contains air. Oxygen present in the air is required by the plant roots and other organisms living in the soil for breathing. Carbon dioxide and nitrogen are also important for the growth of plants.

Water: Water is also a component of soil. Plants absorb water from the soil through their roots. It is also used by soil organisms for different purposes.

Living organisms: Soil contains many living organisms such as earthworms and microorganisms such as bacteria and fungi that help in the formation of humus. Earthworms are called farmers' friend because their movement in the soil causes the soil to turn in and out. This helps in the circulation of air in the soil, which helps in the growth of plants.

Soil is 45% Rock material
25% Air
25% Water
5% Organic material and living organisms

Science in Context

Most of the things around us are made from minerals obtained from soil. We get metals, glass, computer chips, clay-based facial scrubs and many chemicals for preparing medicines from soil.

Revise and Recall

State whether the following statements are true (T) or false (F).

1. The process of the natural breakdown of rocks is known as weathering. ☐
2. Soil is only brown in colour. ☐
3. Humus is the inorganic component of soil. ☐
4. Soil also contains air. ☐
5. Earthworms do not help in the formation of humus. ☐

SOIL PROFILE

a

Soil profile is the term used to describe the layers of soil. There are three layers of soil—topsoil, subsoil and bedrock.

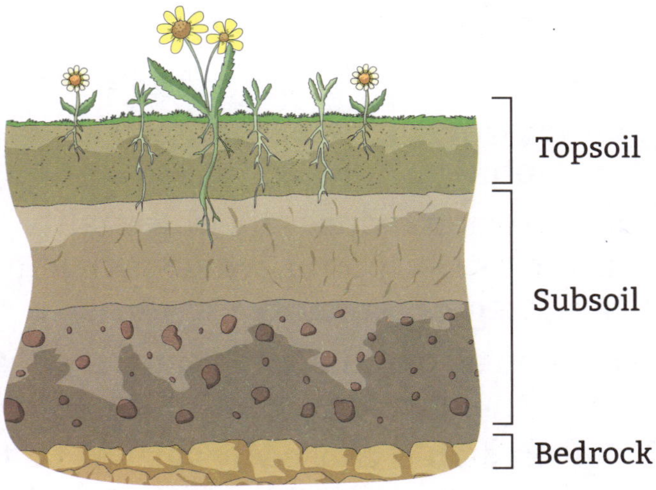

Soil profile

Topsoil: It refers to the uppermost layer of soil, in which the plants grow. This layer contains fine particles such as sand and clay. Topsoil is rich in humus, air and water that are required for the growth of plants.

Subsoil: It is the middle layer of soil under the topsoil. It consists of broken pieces of rock. It is more compact and contains less air but has water. Subsoil contains very less humus compared to the topsoil, making it less fertile. It is lighter in colour than the topsoil.

Bedrock: It is the bottom layer of the soil. This layer contains large pieces of rocks and is very hard. The rocks in this layer are unweathered rocks. There is not much water here.

Soil profile is different in different areas. Climate of the area and time taken for the soil formation affects the soil profile and the soil type.

Types of Soil

There are three main types of soil based on the size, feel and colour of soil particles: clay, silt and sand.

Clay contains particles of fine size. Clayey soil is sticky and holds water well. Cereals grow well in clayey soil.

Science in Context

When clay, silt and sand are mixed properly, loam soil is formed. Loam soil has the benefits of these three types of soil with few of the disadvantages.

Silt contains particles that are bigger than clay but smaller than sand.

Sand contains particles that are bigger than silt. This soil is light and dry. It drains off water very quickly. Coconut trees grow well in sandy soil.

SOIL EROSION

The removal of topsoil by the action of either wind or water is known as **soil erosion**.

Soil erosion reduces the soil quality as the fertile topsoil, which is rich in humus, gets removed.

Erosion also reduces the capacity of the soil to hold water.

Soil erosion is caused by various factors such as heavy rainfall, strong winds, overgrazing of animals and deforestation.

Soil erosion

The maximum erosion occurs due to the force of moving water. Water washes the soil away from a place and makes it unsuitable to grow plants.

SOIL CONSERVATION

a

Prevention of soil erosion is called **soil conservation**. Soil erosion removes the topsoil that contains humus required for maintaining the fertility of soil. Hence, it is important to take some steps to conserve soil.

Ways to Conserve Soil

Plant more trees: The roots of trees hold onto the soil and prevent the erosion of soil.

Trees prevent soil erosion

Avoid overgrazing by cattle: Do not allow cattle to graze in the same area for a long period of time.

Avoid overgrazing

Crop rotation: Growing different types of crops on the same farmland in the successive seasons is called crop rotation.

This practice helps in maintaining the soil fertility.

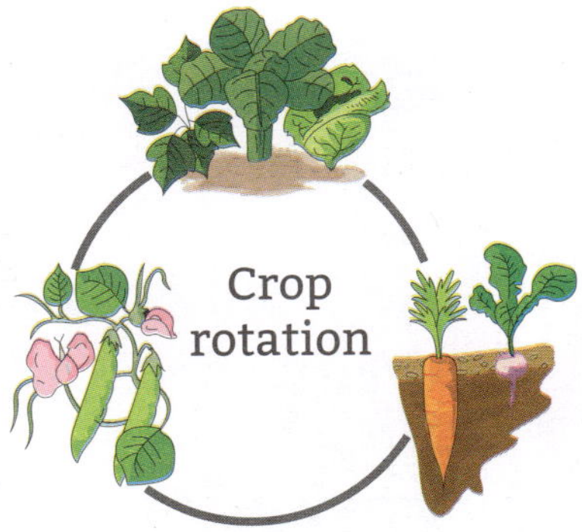

Bunds or embankments: The overflow of water during floods carries away the topsoil. This can be prevented by building embankments or bunds along the riverbanks.

This also prevents damage to the crops during floods.

Terrace or contour farming: Soil in hilly regions can be prevented from being washed away by water if the flow of water is slowed down.

This can be done by creating a series of steps or terraces where the crops are planted. This prevents soil erosion in the hills during heavy rainfall.

Revise and Recall

Fill in the blanks with the correct words.

1. The natural breakdown of rocks is known as____________. (weathering/soil erosion)
2. Growing different types of crops on the same farmland in the successive seasons is called __________. (contour farming/crop rotation)
3. The bottom layer of the soil is called___________. (topsoil/bedrock)
4. The dark brown substance formed due to the decay of dead plants and animals is ____________. (humus/soil creatures)
5. Soil erosion ______________ the soil quality. (reduces/increases)

Keywords

Soil: The topmost layer of the Earth's surface, which consists of sand, remains of dead plants and animals, minerals and some amount of air and water

Weathering: The process of the natural breakdown of rocks into smaller particles

Humus: The dark brown substance formed due to the decay of dead plants and animals

Topsoil: The uppermost layer of soil in which plants grow

Subsoil: The middle layer of soil that contains broken pieces of rocks

Bedrock: The bottom layer of soil that contains large pieces of rocks

Soil erosion: The removal of topsoil by wind or water

Soil conservation: Prevention of soil from erosion

Summary

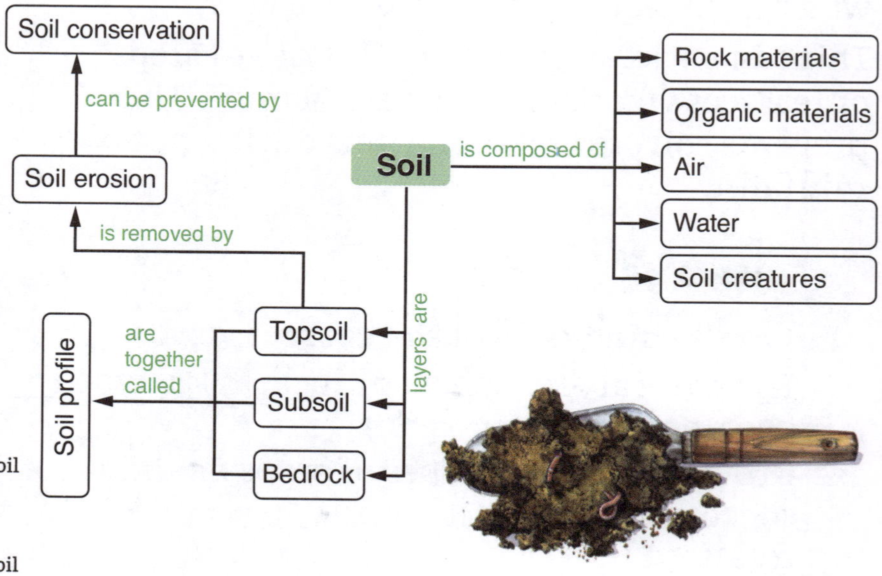

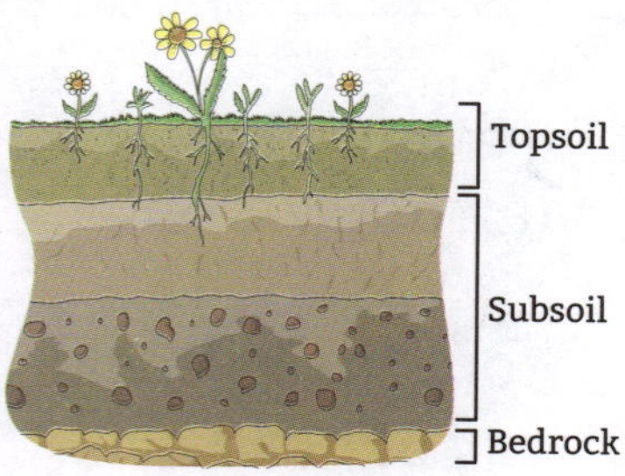

Soil profile

Exercise

W

A. Choose the correct option for each of the following.

ia

1. Contraction and expansion of rocks is due to the action of
   (a) Wind (b) Water (c) Animals (d) Sun
2. Which causes maximum erosion?
   (a) Wind (b) Water
   (c) Overgrazing (d) Deforestation
3. The layer just below the topsoil is called
   (a) Bedrock (b) Clay (c) Gravel (d) Subsoil
4. Which layer of soil is rich in humus?
   (a) Topsoil (b) Subsoil (c) Clay (d) Bedrock
5. Soil erosion usually removes the
   (a) Topsoil (b) Subsoil (c) Bedrock (d) Sandy soil

B. Fill in the blanks with the correct words.

ia

1. __________ need soil to grow. (Animals/Plants)
2. __________ are called farmers' friends. (Earthworms/Frogs)
3. Soil __________ describes the layers of soil. (erosion/profile)
4. The type of soil that holds water well is __________. (clay/sand)

C. State whether the following statements are true (T) or false (F).

ia

1. Formation of soil is a slow process. ☐
2. Humus helps the soil to hold more water. ☐
3. Subsoil contains less air than topsoil. ☐
4. Cereal plants grow well in clayey soil. ☐
5. Farming in hilly regions on a series of steps is called contour farming. ☐

D. Give two examples for each of the following.

1. Components of soil __________ __________
2. Layers of soil __________ __________
3. Causes of soil erosion __________ __________

E. Give reasons for the following.

1. Humus in the soil helps the plants for their growth.
2. Earthworms are called farmers' friend.
3. The subsoil is lighter in colour than the topsoil.
4. Planting more trees prevents soil erosion.
5. Crop rotation helps in maintaining the soil fertility.

F. Answer the following questions briefly.

1. What is weathering?
2. What are the effects of soil erosion?
3. What is crop rotation?
4. What is terrace farming?

G. Answer the following questions.

1. Describe the formation of soil.
2. Compare the four different types of soil.
3. Describe soil profile with the help of a labelled diagram.
4. Write any three ways in which we can prevent soil erosion.

Cognitive Corner

Critical Thinking

1. What type of soil is used for making pots?
2. What type of plants would you grow on a sloping terrain?
3. How do decaying plant and animal remains make the soil fertile?
4. During monsoon, you would have observed many earthworms in the parks or on the roads or at your garden. Can you tell from where these earthworms came?
5. Take a tumbler/vessel and fill half with water. Put one or two dry mud blocks into the water. Do you see bubbles coming up? Where do these bubbles come from? Explain.

Picture Study

Look at the picture given below. Name the three layers of soil in the given boxes. Also, help Mr/Ms Worm to get to the top of the soil surface.

Project

Draw a chart on soil profile. Colour and label the different layers of soil. Display the chart in your class.

Life Skill

Pictures of various substances found in the soil are given. Which of these items will decay and form humus and which will not decay? What will happen if the items do not decay?

Leaf

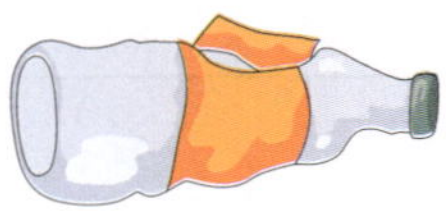
Plastic bottle

Banana peel

Dead bird

Rotten tomato

Tin can

Egg shell

Cloth bag

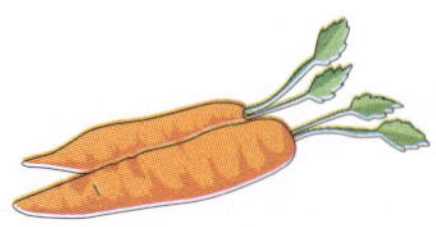
Carrots

Worksheet

Mountain slopes are prone to landslides during heavy rains. Rainwater seeps into the soil and makes the soil and rocks heavy. The Earth's gravity then pulls the slope down. A part of the slope suddenly breaks away and comes crashing down sweeping everything in its path.

The flash floods and landslides of 2013 in Uttarakhand killed thousands of residents and tourists and devastated an entire region. Landslides are a part of natural disasters, but human interference can turn the event into a big disaster.

A. Tick the factors that can prevent landslides. Cross the ones that can make landslides worse.

1. Forest-covered mountain slope. ☐
2. Replacing trees with houses. ☐
3. Building large number of hotels to attract tourists on the slopes. ☐
4. Planting trees to replace the ones cut down for human activities. ☐
5. Using pumps to use the groundwater. ☐

B. What can you do, at your end, to spread awareness about landslides and soil erosion?

____

____

____

____

____

____

____

____

____

____

13 Solids, Liquids and Gases

Learning Checklist

- States of matter
- Changing states of matter
- Dissolving solids in water

Let's Get Started

Look at the objects below and write (S) for solids, (L) for liquids and (G) for gases in each of the boxes provided.

Air ☐

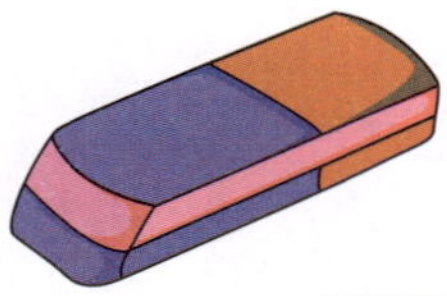

Rubber ☐

Vapour ☐

Milk ☐

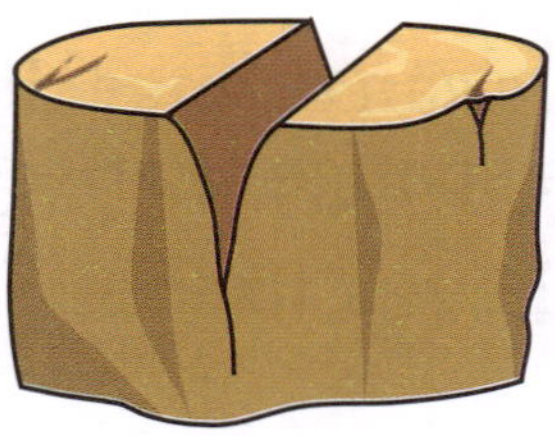

Wood ☐

Oil ☐

We see different types of objects around us, for example, water, air and trees. All these objects are made up of matter.

Anything that has mass and occupies space is called **matter**. The human body is also made up of matter. The air we breathe and the water we drink are also matter.

Let us learn more about matter in this chapter.

STATES OF MATTER

a

Matter exists in three different states—solids, liquids and gases.

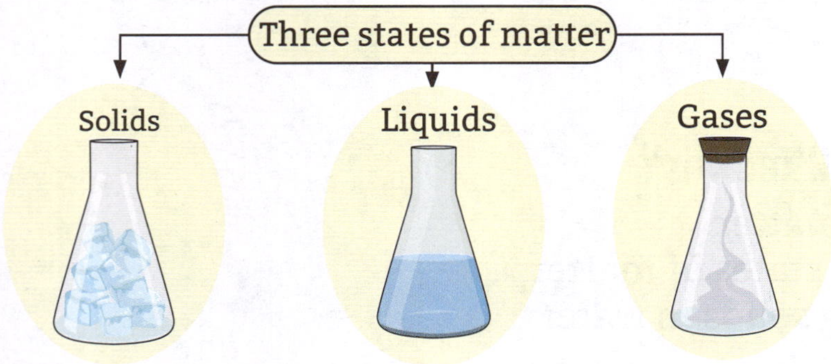

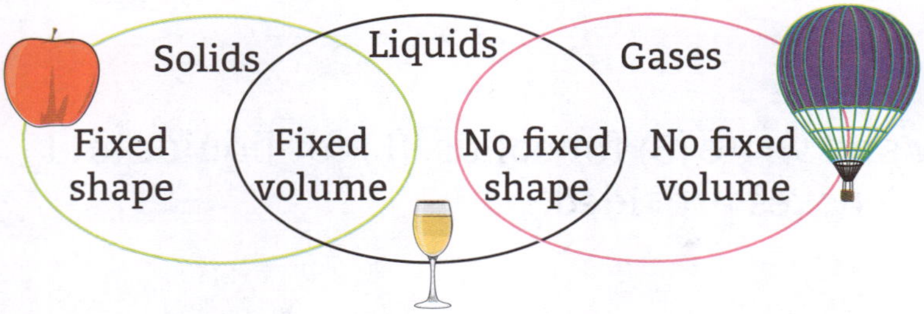

Science in Context

Light and sound are not matter. This is because both light and sound neither have mass, nor do they occupy space.

Solids

In solids, the particles are packed very close to each other. As a result, these particles cannot move around. That is why solids are hard and have a fixed shape, size and volume.

However, if we use force, we can change the shape of some solids. For example, the shape of a sponge changes when we compress it.

Solids cannot flow as they have a fixed shape. Ice, book and pencil are some examples of solids.

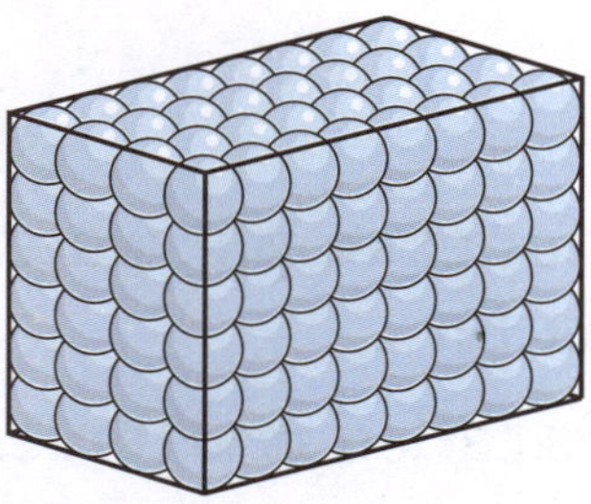

Arrangement of particles in solids

Sofa Ice

Examples of solids

Liquids

In liquids, the particles are not very closely packed and thus can move around. Liquids do not have a fixed shape but have a fixed volume. They can flow and take the shape of the container into which they are poured. Water, milk and oil are some examples of liquids.

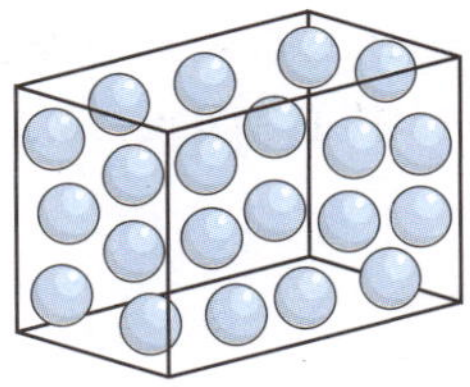

Arrangement of particles in liquids

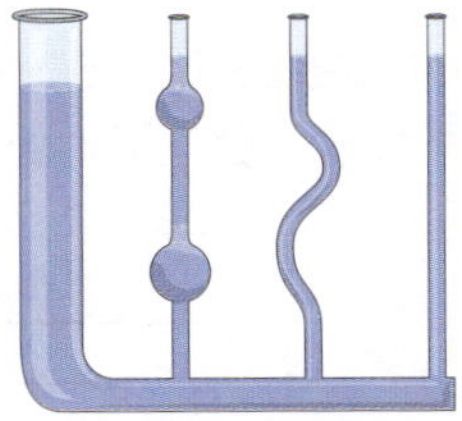

Liquid taking the shape of container

Science in Context

The particles are more tightly packed in solids than in liquids but water is an exception. The particles in ice (solid) have more space between them than the particles in water (liquid).

Gases

In gases, the particles are very loosely packed as compared to solids and liquids. As a result, gas particles can move freely in any direction. They can be compressed very easily and can even flow easily. Gases have neither a fixed shape nor a fixed volume. Gases occupy all the available space in a container. Water vapour, oxygen and nitrogen are some examples of gases.

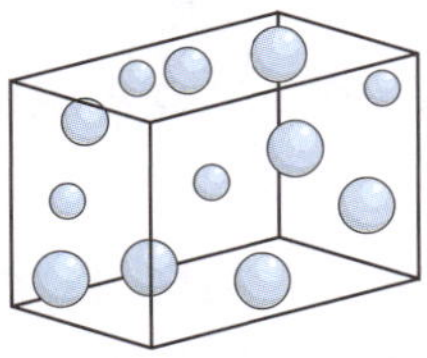

Arrangement of particles in gases

Steam

Air inside balloon

Examples of gases

The table given below shows the differences in the properties of solids, liquids and gases.

Solids	Liquids	Gases
Have fixed shape and volume	Have fixed volume but no fixed shape	No fixed shape and volume
Very less space between the particles	Space between the particles is more than that in solids	Space between the particles is more than that in solids and liquids
Cannot flow	Can flow from a higher level to a lower level	Can flow in all directions

CHANGING STATES OF MATTER

Can we change the state of matter from solid to liquid or from liquid to gas? Let us perform an activity to find out.

Activity 1

Take ice cubes in a beaker and keep it outside for some time. Observe the changes. Then, take water in a pan and heat it. Observe what happens.

From the above activity, it is clear that matter can change from one state to another when it is heated or cooled.

How does this change in state take place?

When a solid is heated, the particles leave their fixed position and move freely. A stage is reached where the particles move so far apart that they change their state, that is, the solid melts and turns into a liquid. This process by which a solid changes into a liquid on heating is called **melting**. When this liquid is cooled, it changes back into the solid state again. This process by which a liquid changes into a solid on cooling is called **freezing**.

When we heat a liquid, the particles start moving faster and further away from each other. A stage is reached where the particles in the liquid move so far away from each other that they change into their gaseous state. This process by which a liquid changes into its gaseous form on heating is called **evaporation**.

When a gas comes in contact with a cold surface, it gets cooled and changes back to liquid. This process by which a gas changes into a liquid on cooling is called **condensation**.

PHYSICAL AND CHEMICAL CHANGES

A change in which no new substance is formed and there is merely a change of state is called a **physical change**. Melting of ice, freezing of water and boiling of water are examples of physical changes.

Physical changes are reversible. In other words, we can get the original substance back even after the change takes place. For example, ice changes to water on heating, but we can get back ice by freezing water.

A **chemical change** is one in which a new substance is formed. This kind of change is irreversible, that is, we cannot get the original substance back once it undergoes a chemical change. Burning of a wax candle and burning of paper are examples of chemical changes.

Revise and Recall

State whether the following statements are true (T) or false (F).

1. The particles in a solid are very closely packed. ☐
2. Solids can be poured into a container. ☐
3. Gas particles cannot move freely. ☐
4. Melting is the process in which a liquid changes into a solid. ☐

DISSOLVING SOLIDS IN WATER

Do solids dissolve[1] in liquids? Let us perform an activity to understand this.

Word Web

[1]**Dissolve**: to mix with a liquid easily

Activity 2

Take a beaker half-filled with water. Add some salt to it and stir continuously. Can you see the salt after a while? Why does the salt seem to disappear when stirred for some time? This is because the salt has dissolved in the water.

Some solids dissolve in liquids. The solid that dissolves in a liquid is called the **solute**. The liquid in which the solute dissolves is called the **solvent**. Water dissolves most solutes. Hence, it is called a *universal solvent*. The liquid obtained after dissolving a solute in a solvent is called a **solution**.

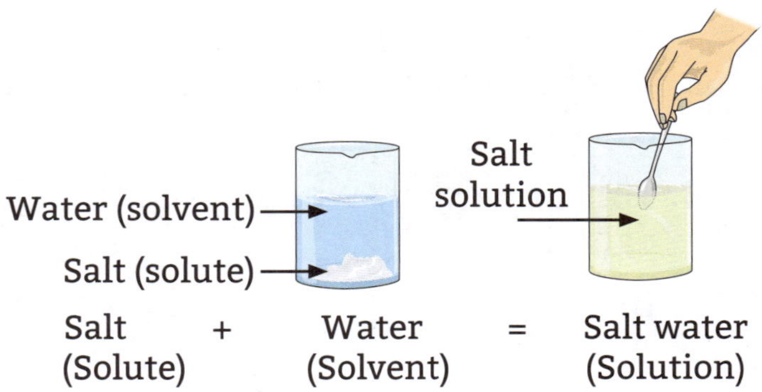

How does a solute dissolve in a solvent?

When we add a solute in a solvent, the solute breaks down into tiny particles that get distributed uniformly among the particles of the solvent. The solute particles occupy the empty spaces between the solvent particles, as shown in the following figure.

Science in Context

The ability of a solvent to dissolve a solute in it can be increased by the following conditions:

- Stirring the solvent so that the solute particles are distributed evenly
- Adding the solute in powdered form
- Heating the solvent makes the solvent particles move faster, enabling the solute to dissolve quickly

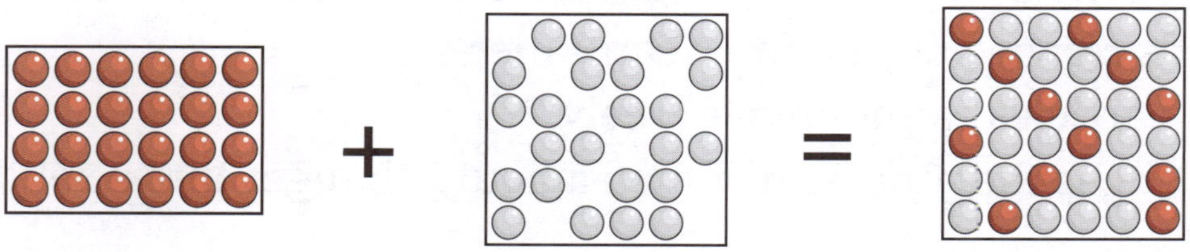

Solute Solvent Solution

Revise and Recall

A. Choose the appropriate word from the text box to fill in the blanks.

condensation	evaporation	solids	freezing	melting

1. The process by which a liquid changes into its gaseous form on heating is called ____________.
2. The process by which a liquid changes into a solid on cooling is called ____________.
3. The process by which a solid changes into a liquid on heating is called ____________.
4. This process by which a gas changes into a liquid on cooling is called ____________.
5. In ____________, there is very less space between the particles.

B. Name the following.

1. Anything that has mass and occupies space ________________
2. Substances that have a fixed shape and volume ________________
3. Substances that have no fixed shape and volume ________________
4. The solid that dissolves in a liquid ________________

Keywords

Melting: The process by which a solid changes into a liquid on heating

Freezing: The process by which a liquid changes into a solid on cooling

Evaporation: The process by which a liquid changes into its gaseous form on heating

Condensation: The process by which a gas changes into a liquid on cooling

Solute: A solid that dissolves in a liquid

Solvent: A liquid in which a solute dissolves

Solution: The liquid obtained after dissolving a solute in a solvent

Summary

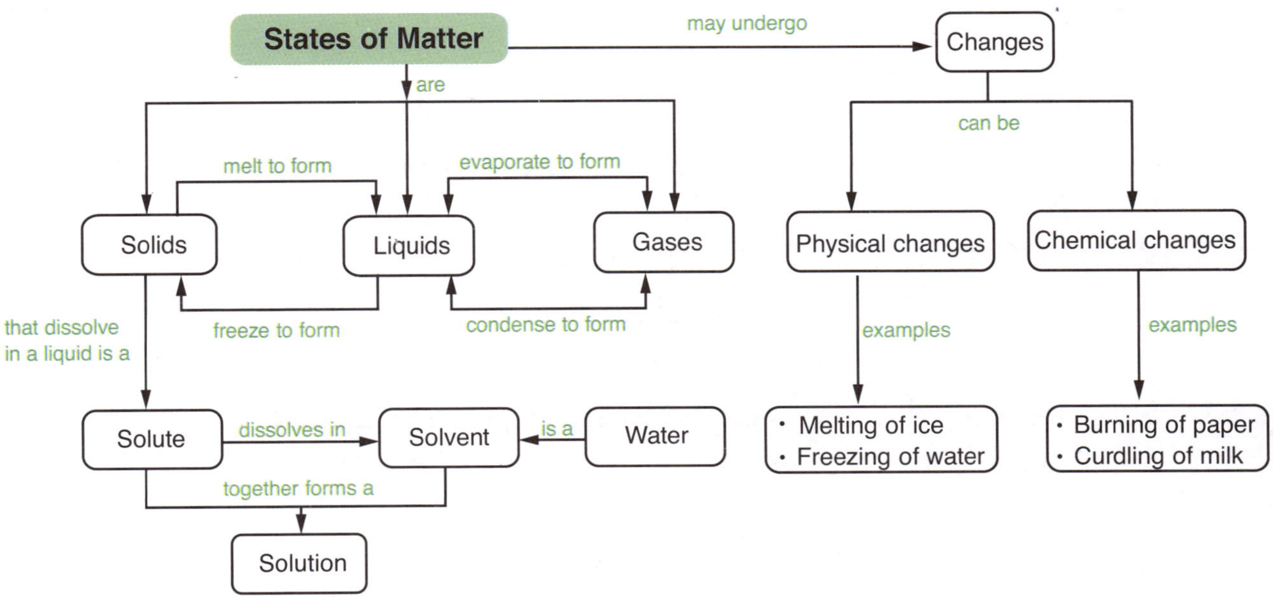

Exercise

W

A. Choose the correct option for each of the following. ia

1. The state of matter in which particles are closely packed
   (a) Solid (b) Liquid (c) Gas (d) All of these
2. Oil is an example of a
   (a) Solid (b) Liquid (c) Gas (d) None of these
3. Which of the following is a gas?
   (a) Ice (b) Milk (c) Steam (d) Juice
4. Identify the substance that exists in all the three states of matter.
   (a) Pencil (b) Water (c) Orange (d) Eraser
5. The solid that dissolves in a liquid is called
   (a) Solvent (b) Season (c) Solution (d) Solute

B. Fill in the blanks with the correct words. ia

1. Matter can exist in __________ states. (three/six)
2. __________ have a fixed shape and volume. (Solids/Liquids)
3. Air is an example of a __________. (solid/gas)
4. Particles in __________ can move freely in any direction. (solids/gases)
5. In a salt solution, __________ is the solvent. (salt/water)

C. State whether the following statements are true (T) or false (F). ia

1. Light is a matter. ☐
2. There is a lot of space between particles in a solid. ☐
3. Liquids take the shape of the container into which they are poured. ☐
4. Water exists in three different forms. ☐
5. Tearing paper is a chemical change. ☐

D. Give reasons for the following.

1. Solids are hard and have a fixed shape, size and volume.
2. Liquids can flow from a higher level to a lower level.
3. Physical changes are reversible.
4. Heating increases the solubility of a liquid.
5. Water is called a universal solvent.

E. Answer the following questions briefly.

1. What is matter? Give two examples.
2. Name the three states of matter.
3. What are solids? Write two examples.
4. What is the difference between a solute and a solvent?
5. What happens when a solute dissolves in a solvent?

F. Answer the following questions.

1. How are solids, liquids and gases different from each other?
2. Explain how matter can change from one state to another.
3. Explain how a solute dissolves in a solvent with the help of a diagram.
4. Explain physical and chemical changes with the help of examples.

Cognitive Corner

Critical Thinking

Monica dissolved two spoonfuls of sugar to a glass of water. She noted that the level of water in the glass remained the same. Can you explain why the water level did not increase?

Picture Study

Observe the pictures shown below. Name the state of matter and write property for each.

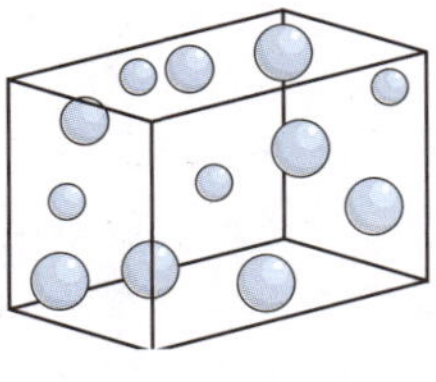

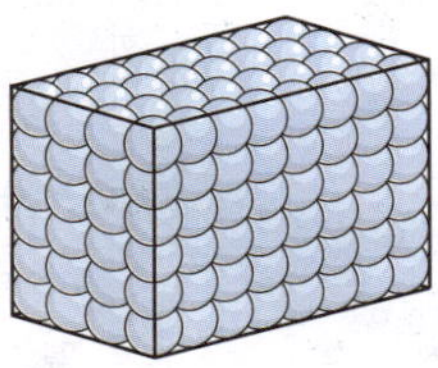

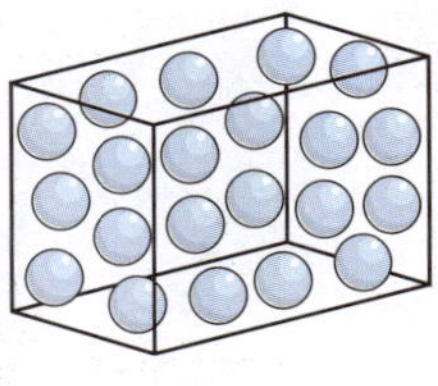

______________ ______________ ______________

Project

1. Make some holes at the base of a plastic bottle. Make one hole at the top too. Fill the bottle with water. What happens when the hole at the top is kept closed and what happens when it is opened? Why does this happen? Record your observation Note down your findings in your science diary.
2. Take balloon dolls of different sizes and shapes. Blow air into them. Then release the air. What happens? Why does this happen? What changes did you observe when air is filled in balloons of different shapes? Does air have a definite shape? Note down your findings in your science diary.

Life Skills

Anjum has lighted an incense stick in her room. Her grandmother, who is in the next room with other family members, has asthma problem and she cannot inhale strong scents. What should Anjum do so that the scent does not reach her grandmother?

Worksheet

Have you ever seen a hot air balloon? Do you know how it works?

Hot air balloon is one of the earliest and the first successful flight technology that could carry humans. It is based on the property that hot air rises.

A hot air balloon has three main parts:

- the burner which heats the air
- the balloon envelope which holds the air and
- the basket which carries the passengers

A. Which other objects use this same property of air? Find any two such objects.

____

____

B. If you were to create a state of matter, what properties would you like it to have? Select a state of matter (solid, liquid or gas) of your choice and fill in the chart given below.

My state of matter: ______________________

What it looks like!	Properties

14 Force, Work and Energy

Learning Checklist

- Types of forces
- Work
- Simple machines
- Energy and its sources

Let's Get Started

You have learned in Class 3 that a push or a pull applied on an object is called force. Force can

- make a body move.
- change the speed and direction of a moving body.
- stop a moving body.
- change the shape of the body.

Look at the pictures given below and write the effects of force shown in each.

1. 

____

____

2. 

____

____

TYPES OF FORCES

a

Force can be of various types, for example, gravitational force, frictional force and muscular force. Let us study more about these forces.

Frictional Force

Friction is the force that slows down the motion of an object. In order to experience frictional force, two surfaces have to be in contact.

Smooth surfaces offer less friction and rough surfaces offer more friction. We find it difficult to walk on an icy surface because the smooth surface of the ice provides very less friction. Walking on a concrete road is easier because the rough surface of the concrete provides ample friction that gives us a good grip on the ground.

Science in Context

In the absence of friction, an object in motion will continue to be in motion forever.

Ice (smooth surface) offers less friction

Activity 1

Aim: To understand that smooth surfaces offer lesser friction than rough surfaces

Materials required: 1 matchbox, 1 metre thread, smooth table and soil

Procedure:

1. Take a matchbox and tie the thread around it.
2. Try pulling the box first on the plane table with the help of a thread.
3. Repeat the process on a table that is spread with soil.

Observation: You will find it difficult to pull the box when soil is spread on the table.

Conclusion: The table spread with soil offers more friction because the surface becomes rough compared to the table surface without soil.

Gravitational Force

When we throw an object upwards, no matter how high it goes, it always falls back to the Earth's surface. This is due to the force applied by the Earth on the object called **gravitational force**.

Gravity or gravitational force always pulls the objects towards the centre of the Earth.

An object thrown up always comes down

Science in Context

One day, Sir Isaac Newton, a great scientist, was visiting an apple orchard. He saw an apple falling from a tree. This made him think and he discovered gravitational force and introduced it to the world.

Muscular Force

Muscular force is applied when we use our muscles. For example, lifting a bucket of water. A weightlifter lifts heavy weights with his arms using muscular force.

Muscular force

Work

In science, **work** is said to be done when a force applied on an object makes the object move along the direction of the applied force.

According to the definition, if an object does not move even after a force is applied, then no work is said to be done. For example, if a boy is pushing a wall, no matter how hard he pushes, the wall will not move. In this case, we say that no work has been done.

Revise and Recall

Fill in the blanks with the correct words.

1. In order to experience frictional force, minimum _______ surfaces have to be in contact. (1/2)
2. Smooth surfaces offer _______ friction comparing to rough surfaces. (less/more)
3. Gravity or gravitational force is always a __________. (pull/push)
4. __________ is applied when we use our muscles. (Muscular force/Gravitational force)
5. Gravitational force was discovered by _______________. (Sir Isaac Newton/Galileo Galilei)

SIMPLE MACHINES

a

Machines help us by making our work easy. For example, we use a spoon to open the tight lid of a can or scissors to cut a thread. The simple tools we use to make our day-to-day work easy are called **simple machines**.

Simple machines are of six types. Let us learn about them.

Lever: Lever is a simple machine used to cut things, lift weights and open lids. Some examples of levers are scissors, bottle openers and see-saws.

Pulley: Pulley is a simple machine with a wheel and a rope, used to raise, lower and move things. A pulley is used to draw a bucket of water from inside a well.

A see-saw

A woman drawing water from a well using a pulley

Inclined plane: Inclined plane is a sloping surface on which objects can be pushed up or down. For example, new cars or carton boxes are loaded on trucks using inclined planes.

Wheel and axle: How are the two wheels in the front or the back of the vehicles connected? The wheels have a rod between them, which acts as a connector. This rod is called the **axle**. When the axle moves, the wheels also move. Wheel and axle make it easy to move heavy things.

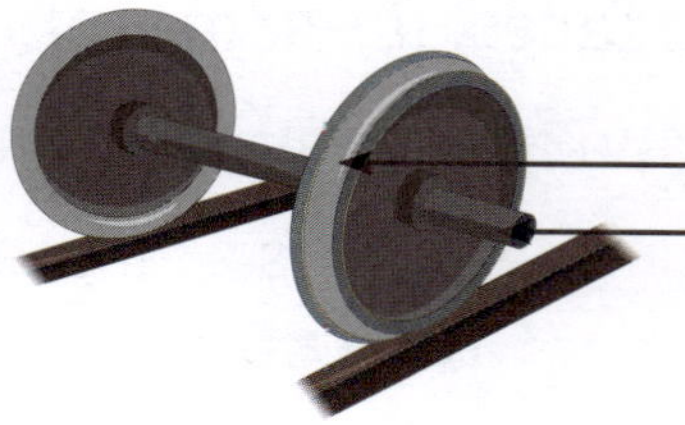

Wedge: Wedge is a simple machine with two slanting surfaces and a sharp edge. Wedges are used to cut things apart. For example, a knife is used to cut vegetables and an axe is used to cut wood.

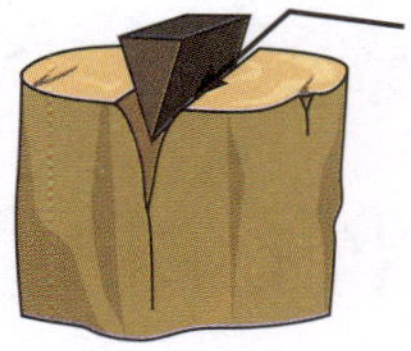

Screw: Screw is a simple machine which is an inclined plane wound around a straight rod. Screws have a cylindrical shape with a sharp edge and a blunt circular top. Screws can be turned by using a screwdriver. They are used to join or attach things. They are used in making furniture and in fixing doors to a frame or a wall.

Screw

ENERGY AND ITS SOURCES

In order to do work, energy is required. **Energy** is defined as the ability to do work.

There are various forms of energy such as electrical, heat, magnetic, sound, light and chemical energy. All these energies are interrelated because energy can be converted from one form to another. You will learn more about these energies in detail in your higher classes.

Light energy

Chemical energy

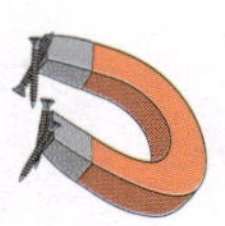
Magnetic energy

Sound energy

Electrical energy

Heat energy

Sources of Energy

Living organisms get energy from the food that they eat, whereas machines use energy from sources such as fuel (petrol, diesel) and electricity.

There are many natural sources of energy such as the sun, wind, water and the Earth.

Solar Energy: The sun is the ultimate source of energy on the Earth. Energy from the sun is called **solar energy**. Devices such as solar heaters and solar cookers use solar energy. Solar energy is also used to generate electricity. Plants use solar energy to carry out photosynthesis.

Wind Energy: Energy generated from the moving air is called **wind energy**. Windmills are devices that are used to generate energy from the wind.

Water Energy: Moving streams of water carry a lot of energy. We build dams to store water from rivers. The stored water is allowed to fall with huge force from a height on turbines that rotate and generate electricity. This energy is also called **hydroelectric energy**.

Earth: Energy obtained from the hot interior of the Earth is called **geothermal energy**.

Solar heater

Windmills

Dam

Renewable Sources of Energy

Some energy sources can be renewed and do not get exhausted[1] easily. These are called **renewable sources** of energy. Examples of renewable sources of energy are the sun, wind and water.

Word Web

[1]**Exhausted**: completely used up

Non-renewable Sources of Energy

Energy sources that cannot be renewed easily and will get exhausted one day are called **non-renewable sources** of energy, for example, coal, petrol and wood. We should use renewable resources more often and minimize the use of non-renewable resources.

Keywords

Force: A push or a pull applied on an object

Friction: The force that slows down the motion of an object when two bodies are in contact

Gravity: Force that pulls the objects towards the centre of the Earth

Work: Work is said to be done if a force applied on an object makes that object move along the direction of the force

Machine: Machines are devices that make our work easy

Energy: Ability to do work

Solar energy: Energy from the sun

Wind energy: Energy from the blowing wind

Geothermal energy: Heat energy obtained from the interior of the Earth

Renewable sources of energy: The sources of energy that can be renewed and do not get used up easily

Non-renewable sources of energy: Those sources that cannot be renewed easily and will get exhausted one day

Summary

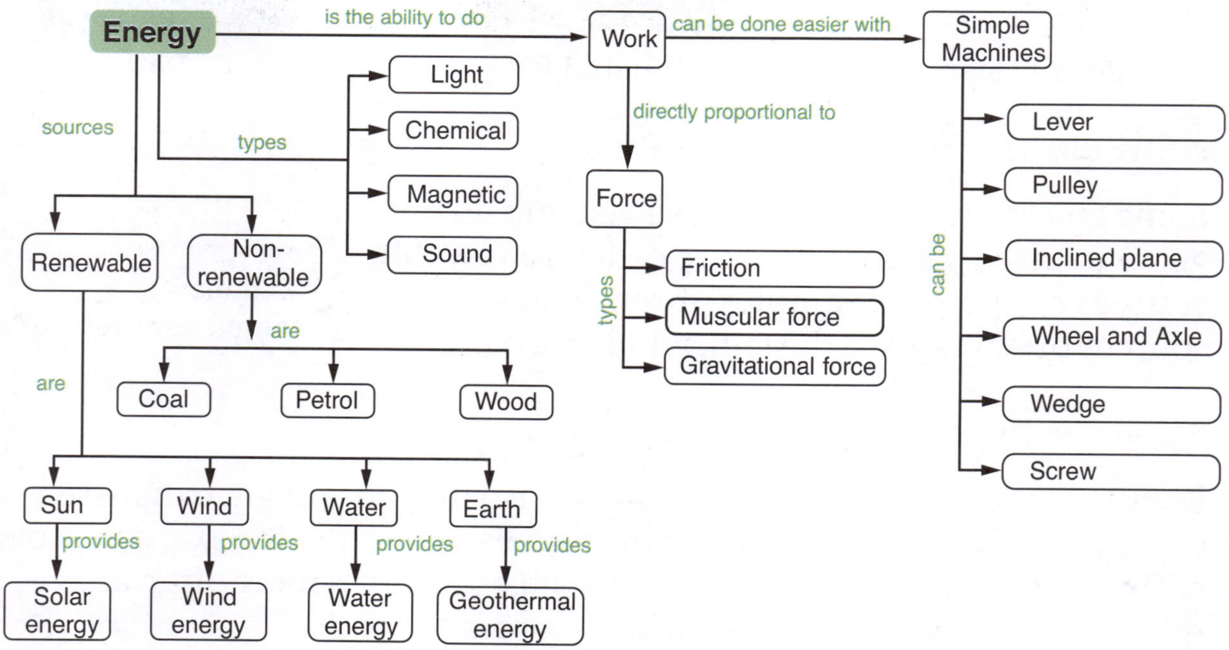

Exercise

A. Choose the correct option for each of the following.

1. The ability to do work is called
   (a) Energy (b) Work (c) Force (d) Machine
2. Identify the simple machine that is a form of two inclined planes joined together.
   (a) Wedge (b) Screw (c) Lever (d) Pulley
3. Which among the following is a source of solar energy?
   (a) Moon (b) Wind (c) Sun (d) Water
4. Which of these is a renewable source of energy?
   (a) Coal (b) Wood (c) Sun (d) Petrol

B. Fill in the blanks with the correct words.

1. Frictional force __________ the motion of an object. (slows down/helps)
2. Gravity and __________ are the two natural forces. (muscular force/friction)
3. We use __________ to make our work easy. (machines/muscles)
4. Windmills are used to extract energy from __________ . (wind/water)
5. __________ can change from one form to another. (Energy/Force)

C. State whether the following statements are true (T) or false (F).

1. Force applied by our muscles is called muscular force. ☐
2. Gravity is a type of friction. ☐
3. Work is done only if force is applied. ☐
4. Levers are slanting surfaces used to push or pull heavy objects to a certain height. ☐
5. The energy that we obtain from flowing water is called solar energy. ☐

D. Give one word for the following.

1. The force that always slows down the motion of objects ____________
2. The force that attracts objects to the Earth's surface ____________
3. The natural energy used by the green leaves to prepare their food ____________
4. The heat energy obtained from the Earth ____________

E. Give reasons for the following.

1. We find it difficult to walk on a wet surface.
2. When we throw an object upwards, it always falls back to the Earth's surface.
3. New cars or carton boxes are loaded on trucks using inclined planes.
4. We must reduce the use of coal and petroleum.
5. The sun is the ultimate source of energy on the Earth.

F. Answer the following questions briefly.

1. Define force.
2. What is a machine?
3. Give two examples of lever.
4. Name any two forms of energy.

G. Answer the following questions.

1. What is friction and how is it useful to us?
2. Under what condition do we consider work to be done?
3. Define energy and explain the various sources of energy.

Cognitive Corner

Critical Thinking

1. What will happen to a body in motion in the absence of friction?
2. A coolie is standing with a heavy luggage on his head. Is he doing any work?
3. We should switch over to energy sources such as the sun and the wind. Why?

Picture Study

Which among the following is an example of a wedge? Name the other simple machines.

(a) 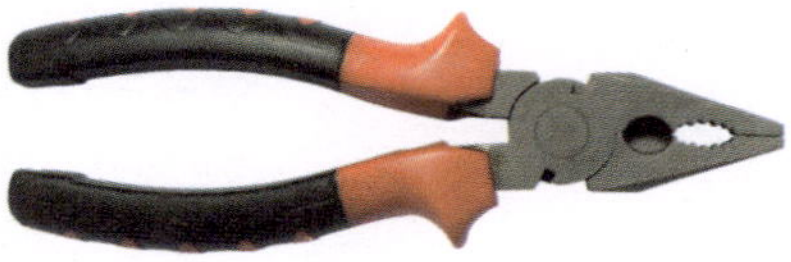 ________________

(b) 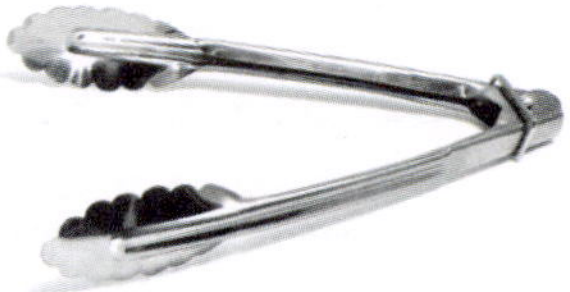 ________________

(c)  ________________

Project

1. Make a list of the different forms of energy being used at your home. Identify which form is being used the most. Compare your list with your classmates.
2. Make a chart on the devices that help in generating energy from natural sources.

   Include the name (and picture) of the source from which each of devices extracts energy. Mention the benefits and harmful effects of using such devices.

Life Skills

You are approached by two different people for help. You need to think and suggest appropriate solutions to both of them.

(a) Person 1: This person needs to load some heavy boxes onto a truck, but he is unable to lift them up on his own. He finds some wooden planks, a wedge and a pulley around. Which of these can he use to load the boxes? Guide him appropriately.

(b) Person 2: This person needs some hot water to drink. His gas stove is not working. He has a vessel that has a glass lid and also a glass of water. Guide him to use the available materials to get hot water.

12 RESPONSIBLE CONSUMPTION AND PRODUCTION

Worksheet

Natural resources such as sun, wind, water and the Earth are renewable. However, if we do not use it wisely, these resources may get exhausted someday.

How can you take part in using these resources wisely? Write down a few remedial measures to save these different resources.

Collins

Adheres to National Education Policy
PREPARATORY STAGE

SUPPLEMENTARY BOOKLET

4

Enhanced Science Now

Series Editor | Jyothsna Natraj

About the STEAM Activities

In the 21st century where the world is rapidly changing with sudden disruptions and unexpected real-world problems, being skilled in just one stream may not be enough. Many real-world problems can be solved only through interdisciplinary approach. Moreover, educationists have been emphasizing on the importance of subject integration and cross-curricular links. **Science**, **technology**, **engineering**, **arts** and **maths** (**STEAM**) education is one such approach where the integration of these five disciplines is utilized to solve real-world problems. Through this approach, a variety of skills such as critical thinking, creativity, innovation, communication, collaboration and entrepreneurship can be applied to make the students ready for the future, where these skills would be applicable in any field of study.

Students need to be introduced to STEAM education early on in life while their mind is still full of curiosity and imagination. STEAM education would not only help in producing tomorrow's designers and engineers, it would also help develop innovative mindsets and the ability to solve real-world problems. This would bring the students one step closer to becoming innovators or creators, not just passive consumers.

This supplementary booklet which comes along with ***Enhanced Science Now*** series, aims to introduce STEAM education to students from classes 1 to 8. There are two problems, based on ***real-world contexts***, in each booklet. The contexts have been carefully designed and mapped directly with the syllabus of each class. The students would be applying interdisciplinary concepts they have learnt in a class to find solution to the given problems. With each problem, research tips have been given to help in the initiation of idea. Clear directives have been given for students to identify the problem, research and record data, record their thinking, sketch their ideas, make observations and improve their design or solution as they work through creating the design or solving the problem.

We hope the students, while applying the concepts they have learnt to solve the real-world problems, would find their learning meaningful and thus be inspired to become future problem solvers, critical thinkers, innovators or inventors.

Content Developed by Excelsoft Technologies Pvt Ltd.

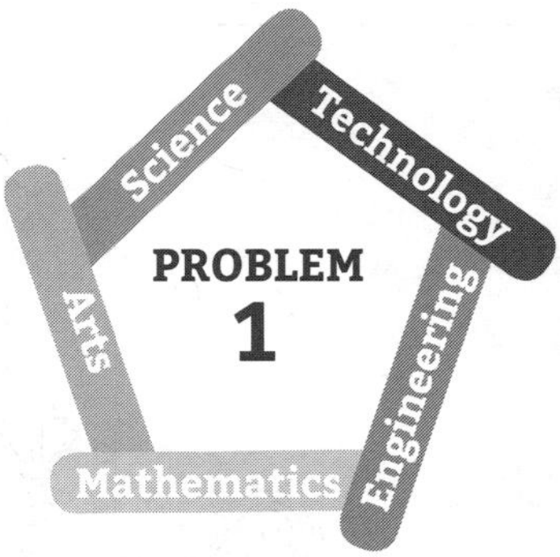

Nungsang's science teacher was discussing about the motion of the Earth around the sun and how day and night occur. He also mentioned about the tilt of the Earth's axis and the occurrence of seasons. Nungsang was very excited and decided to search for more information on the same. He wanted to make a model to demonstrate the occurrence of day and night and the reason for the change of seasons.

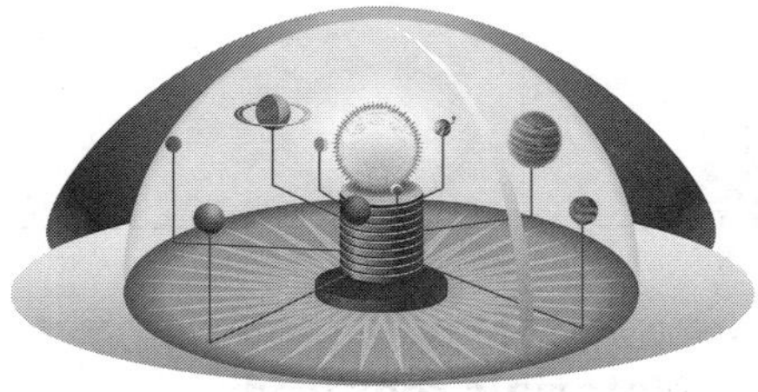

Help Nungsang design and construct a model to demonstrate the phenomena mentioned above.

Statement of the problem:

____

____

____

____

____

Research tips:

1. Motion of the Earth around the sun
2. Motion of the Earth about its axis
3. Tilt of the Earth's axis.
4. Occurrence of day and night
5. How seasons occur

Gather information relevant for this problem.

1. ______________________________
   ____
2. ______________________________
   ____
3. ______________________________
   ____
4. ______________________________
   ____

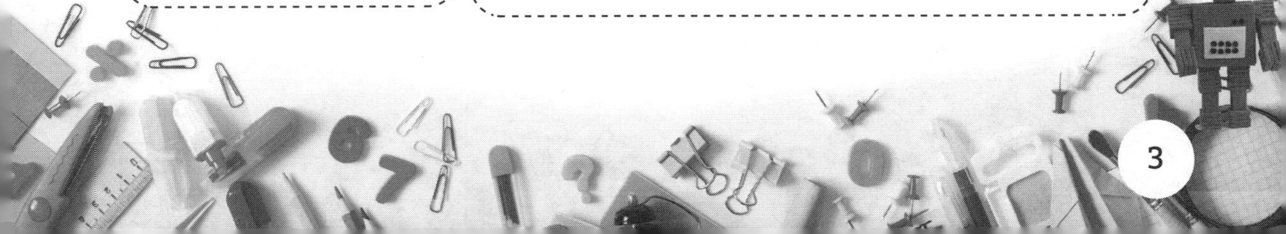

Draw/Sketch your design.

Materials required:

____

____

____

____

____

Construction (Write down the steps to build your design):

1. ______________________________

____

2. ______________________________

____

3. ______________________________

____

4. ______________________________

____

Implementation of the prototype (Try out your model):

Step 1: ____________________

Step 2: ____________________

Step 3: ____________________

Step 4: ____________________

Observation (What worked? What did not work?):

____

____

____

____

____

Scope for improvement (How can you make it better?):

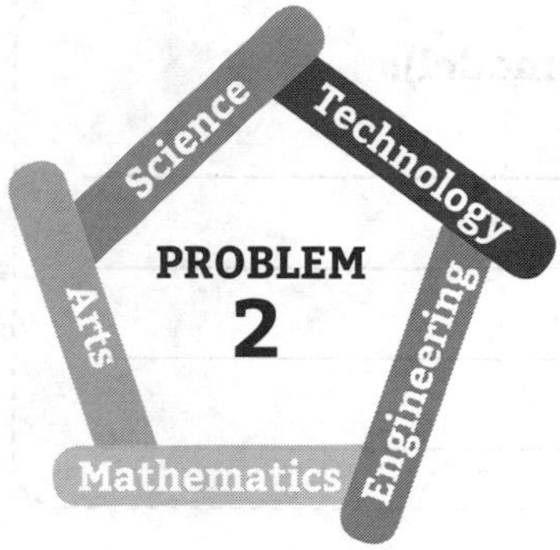

Ann's science teacher was discussing about natural disasters such as earthquakes, cyclones and tsunami. During the class, they discussed about the seismic waves produced during an earthquake and how these waves cause destruction to buildings and bridges.

Ann researched further on earthquake and learned that specially designed buildings can reduce the effect caused by an earthquake; hence, minimizing the damage to life and things inside the building.

She wants to design and construct an earthquake-proof house and demonstrate the same in her class.

Help Ann design and construct the model.

Statement of the problem:

____

____

____

____

____

Research tips:

1. How earthquake occurs
2. Seismic waves
3. Reducing the effects of an earthquake
4. Earthquake-proof buildings
5. Construction materials for earthquake-proof buildings

Gather information relevant for this problem.

1. ______________________________
   ____
2. ______________________________
   ____
3. ______________________________
   ____
4. ______________________________
   ____

Draw/Sketch your design.

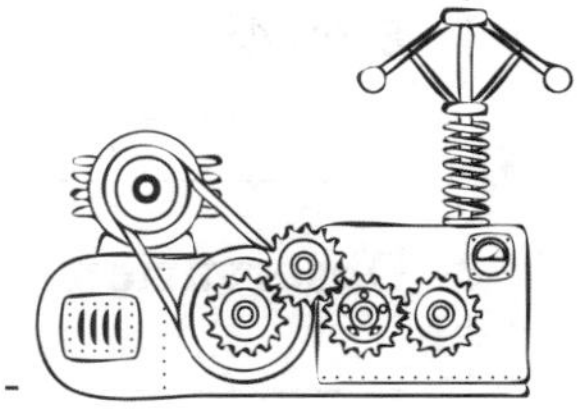

Materials required:

____

____

____

____

____

Construction (Write down the steps to build your design):

1. ____

   ____

2. ____

   ____

3. ____

   ____

4. ____

   ____

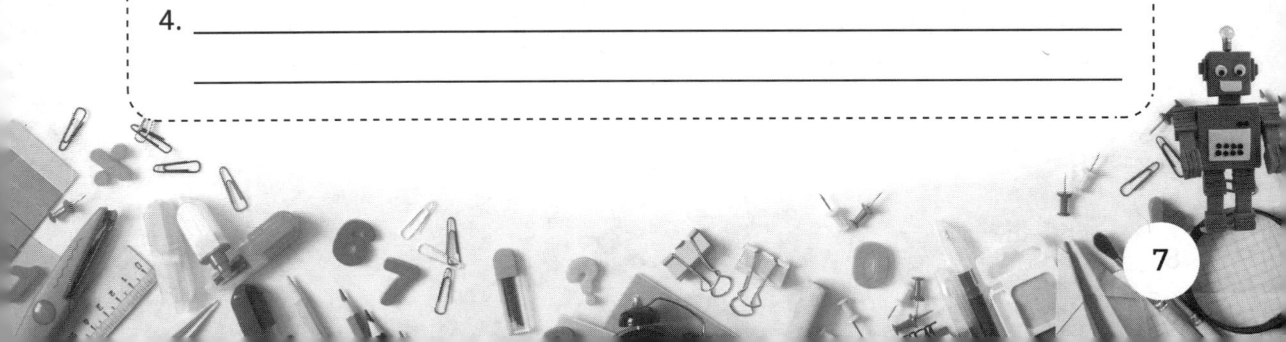

Implementation of the prototype (Try out your model):

Step 1: ____________________

Step 2: ____________________

Step 3: ____________________

Step 4: ____________________

Observation (What worked? What did not work?):

____

____

____

____

____

Scope for improvement (How can you make it better?):

STEAM Vocabulary

Construction: The way in which a thing is built or put together

Implementation: Trying out/carrying out/experimenting

Prototype: A working model of a new product/new version of an old product

Scope: Possibility

Assessment 1

CHAPTERS 1–4
(Maximum Marks = 25)

A. Choose the correct option for each of the following. (7 × 1 = 7)

1. Which of the following is not required by plants to prepare their food?
   (a) Sunlight (b) Water (c) Carbon dioxide (d) Oxygen
2. Which part of a plant holds the leaf to the stem?
   (a) Vein (b) Midrib (c) Petiole (d) Root
3. Which of the following animal reproduces by laying eggs?
   (a) Deer (b) Frog (c) Hippopotamus (d) Rabbit
4. The large cluster of eggs of frog is called
   (a) Tadpole (b) Maggot (c) Nymph (d) Spawn
5. Duckweed, water lettuce and water hyacinth are examples of
   (a) Desert plants (b) Terrestrial plants
   (c) Plants grown on plains (d) Floating plants
6. The area where mangroves grow
   (a) Marshy area (b) Clayey area (c) Sandy area (d) Desert area
7. Which of the following parasite lives inside the body of its host?
   (a) Ticks (b) Tapeworm (c) Lice (d) Fleas

B. State whether the following statements are true (T) or false (F). (6 × 1 = 6)

1. The major products of photosynthesis are carbon dioxide and water. ☐
2. The chain that shows how one organism depends on another for food is called food chain. ☐
3. Floating plants do not have a stem to fix them to the soil bed. ☐
4. Cattail is an emergent plant. ☐
5. Fish lay only one egg in water at a time. ☐
6. Penguin is a terrestrial animal that lives in polar regions. ☐

C. Replace the underlined word with the correct word. (6 × 1 = 6)

1. The midrib branches into smaller structures called <u>arteries</u>.
2. The animals on which the parasite depends for nutrition are called <u>carnivores</u>.
3. <u>Dolphin</u> is the largest mammal.
4. Animals that eat only plants are called <u>omnivores</u>.
5. Animals that live in water are called <u>arboreal</u> animals.
6. The yellow-coloured substance present in an egg is called <u>albumen</u>.

D. Answer each of the following questions in one word. (6 × 1 = 6)

1. What is the other name for winter sleep?
2. What is the term used for the animals that may disappear soon from the Earth?

3. Name the process of shedding of skin in some animals.
4. Name the process by which living organisms produce young ones of their own kind.
5. What is the other name for summer sleep?
6. Name the tiny openings in a leaf through which plants take in carbon dioxide.

Assessment 2

CHAPTERS 5-7
(Maximum Marks = 25)

A. Pick the odd one out from each of the following groups of words. **(7 × 1 = 7)**

1. Heart	Blood	Blood vessels	Lungs
2. Artery	Vein	Capillary	Heart
3. Kidney	Uterus	Urinary bladder	Urethra
4. Crown	Neck	Root	Stem
5. Small intestine	Stomach	Blood	Saliva
6. Yogurt	Cheese	Tomato soup	Milk
7. Sapling	Canning	Jellying	Drying

B. State whether the following statements are true (T) or false (F). **(6 × 1 = 6)**

1. Kidneys remove harmful wastes such as urine and excess salts from our body. ☐
2. Ureters are the tubes that carry urine from the kidneys to the urinary bladder. ☐
3. Saliva makes the food soft and easy to swallow. ☐
4. Liver and pancreas are not the part of the digestive system. ☐
5. All food items contain the same nutrients. ☐
6. We need at least 6-8 hours of sleep in a day. ☐

C. Fill in the blanks using the correct words. **(6 × 1 = 6)**

1. Arteries, veins and capillaries are ____________. (blood vessels/cells)
2. The heart is a ____________ organ that pumps blood to all the parts of the body. (muscular/non-muscular)
3. The undigested food passes into the ____________ intestine where extra water and minerals are absorbed. (large/small)
4. ____________ are the microbes that grow on dead and decaying matter. (Fungi/Virus)
5. The process of treating food to prevent it from getting spoilt is called ____________. (balanced diet/preservation)
6. Our body loses water by ____________. (eating/sweating)

D. Name the following. **(6 × 1 = 6)**

1. The organ system that helps to remove wastes from our body
2. The microscopic living beings found in rod, round or spiral shapes
3. The organ through which undigested food passes before it is removed from the body
4. The method of preserving food using sugar syrup
5. The very long, coiled tube connected to the stomach where digestion is completed
6. The meal that contains all the nutrients required by the body in the right proportion

Assessment 3

CHAPTERS 8-11
(Maximum Marks = 25)

A. Choose the correct option for each of the following. **(7 × 1 = 7)**

1. Which among the following is a satellite?
   (a) Sun (b) Mercury (c) Moon (d) Pluto
2. Identify the dwarf planet among the following.
   (a) Venus (b) Mercury (c) Neptune (d) Pluto
3. Meena washed and spread the following clothes on a string. Which of them would dry the fastest?
   (a) Cotton tops (b) Nylon T-shirt
   (c) Woollen sweater (d) Silk bedspread
4. The cultivation of silkworm to obtain silk is known as
   (a) Agriculture (b) Apiculture (c) Sericulture (d) Horticulture
5. Forest fires occur mostly during
   (a) Summer (b) Winter (c) Spring (d) Rainy season
6. Clouds are formed when water vapour
   (a) Condenses (b) Evaporates (c) Melts (d) Freezes
7. The process in which solid substances are allowed to settle at the bottom of a liquid is known as
   (a) Decantation (b) Filtration (c) Sedimentation (d) Boiling

B. State whether the following statements are true (T) or false (F). **(6 × 1 = 6)**

1. Moon is the natural satellite of the Earth. ☐
2. Nylon, polyester and terylene are some examples of natural fibres. ☐
3. The materials used for making clothes are called fabrics. ☐
4. Reducing the use of paper can save trees. ☐
5. The movement of the Earth around the sun is known as rotation. ☐
6. The Earth is always in a state of motion. ☐

C. Replace the underlined word in each of the following sentences with the correct word. **(6 × 1 = 6)**

1. <u>Mercury</u> is the hottest planet in the solar system.
2. Wool and silk are <u>plant</u> fibres.
3. We sweat a lot in <u>winter</u>.
4. <u>Animals</u> provide us clean air to breathe.
5. <u>Afforestation</u> leads to the shortage of food and water for the wild animals.
6. <u>Gases</u> have fixed volume but no fixed shape.

D. Name the following. **(6 × 1 = 6)**

1. The huge balls of hot gases that give out heat and light continuously
2. The smallest planet in the solar system
3. The balls that are placed between the folds of the woollen clothes to protect them from insects
4. The destruction of forests by cutting down a large number of trees
5. Trees give us this for making furniture
6. The movement of cool air from land towards the sea during night

Assessment 4

CHAPTERS 12–14
(Maximum Marks = 25)

A. Pick the odd one out from each of the following groups of words. **(7 × 1 = 7)**

1.	Gravel	Clay	Loam	Humus
2.	Topsoil	Subsoil	Bottom soil	Bedrock
3.	Crop rotation	Overgrazing	Deforestation	Strong winds
4.	Ice	Apple	Steam	Water
5.	Solute	Solid	Solvent	Solution
6.	Friction	Solar	Wind	Geothermal
7.	Scissors	Knife	Bottle opener	See-saw

B. State whether the following statements are true (T) or false (F). **(6 × 1 = 6)**

1. Soil erosion removes the topsoil. ☐
2. Tearing of paper is a physical change. ☐
3. The solid that dissolves in a liquid is called solvent. ☐
4. In solids, there is more space between the particles than in liquids. ☐
5. Gravity is a natural force. ☐
6. We slip while walking on a smooth surface because it offers more friction. ☐

C. Fill in the blanks using the correct words. **(6 × 1 = 6)**

1. ______________ is the layer of soil that contains most of the humus. (Topsoil/ Subsoil)
2. Growing different types of plants in the same area in the successive seasons is called ______________. (crop revolution/crop rotation)
3. The process by which a liquid changes into its gaseous form is called ______________. (melting/evaporation)
4. Water drops seen on the leaves during early morning is an example of ______________. (evaporation/condensation)
5. Green leaves use ______________ energy to prepare their own food. (wind/ solar)
6. Geothermal energy is obtained from the ______________. (Earth/sun)

D. Answer the following questions in one word. **(6 × 1 = 6)**

1. Which type of soil is sticky and holds more water?
2. Which state of matter cannot flow?
3. By which process does a solid change into a liquid?
4. Name the source of solar energy.
5. Name the device used to obtain energy from moving wind.
6. Name the form of energy obtained from the hot interior of the Earth.

Comprehensive Assessment 1

CHAPTERS 1–7
(Maximum Marks = 50)

A. Name the following. **(10 × 1 = 10)**

1. The process of treating food to prevent spoilage
2. A meal that contains carbohydrates, proteins, fats, minerals, vitamins, water and fibre in the right proportion
3. The other name for aestivation
4. The flat part of a leaf
5. A special feature that allows a plant or an animal to survive in its habitat
6. The process in which one of the parent birds sits on the eggs until they hatch
7. The smallest blood vessels
8. The tubes that carry urine from the kidneys to the urinary bladder
9. The visible part of a tooth
10. The set of teeth used to cut and bite food

B. In each of the following questions, two choices are correct. Identify the correct choices. **(9 × 2 = 18)**

1. Sameeksha fell down the stairs and fractured her elbow. Which of the following food items should be included in her diet to strengthen her bones?
   (a) Milk (b) Butter (c) Fish (d) Nuts (e) Potato (f) Rice
2. Identify the amphibians from the following.
   (a) Lion (b) Camel (c) Frog (d) Whale (e) Bat (f) Salamander
3. The midrib and veins of a leaf help in
   (a) Transportation of water (b) Giving support to the leaf
   (c) Trapping insects (d) Trapping sunlight
   (e) Transportation of food (f) Reproduction of plants
4. Chlorophyll is necessary for
   (a) Trapping sunlight (b) Transporting water
   (c) Preparing food (d) Attracting insects
   (e) Preparing nectar (f) Adding colour to the flowers
5. Identify the types of aquatic plants from the following.
   (a) Terrestrial plants (b) Floating plants (c) Fixed plants
   (d) Ornamental plants (e) Insectivores plants (f) Non-green plants
6. Adaptations found in desert plants
   (a) Small roots (b) Large flowers (c) Spines
   (d) Thick stem (e) Many leaves (f) Juicy fruits
7. Identify the animals that do not reproduce by laying eggs.
   (a) Fish (b) Housefly (c) Cow
   (d) Butterfly (e) Cockroach (f) Whale
8. The organs of the excretory system are
   (a) Urinary bladder (b) Kidney (c) Heart
   (d) Blood vessels (e) Brain (f) Ears
9. The blood vessels consist of
   (a) Arteries (b) White blood cells (c) Capillaries
   (d) Bone cells (e) Joints (f) Dead cells

C. Label the diagrams. **(2 × 3 = 6)**

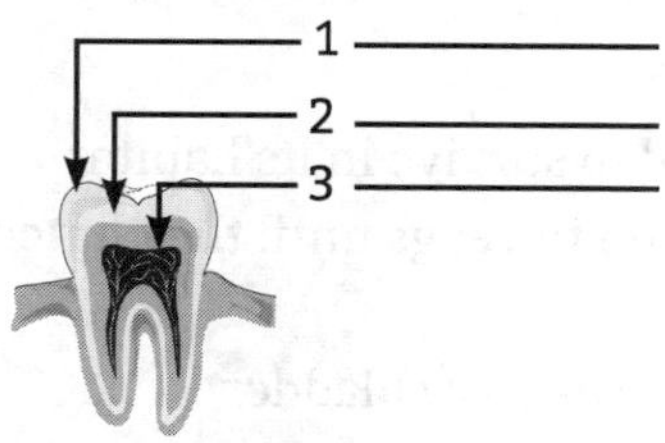

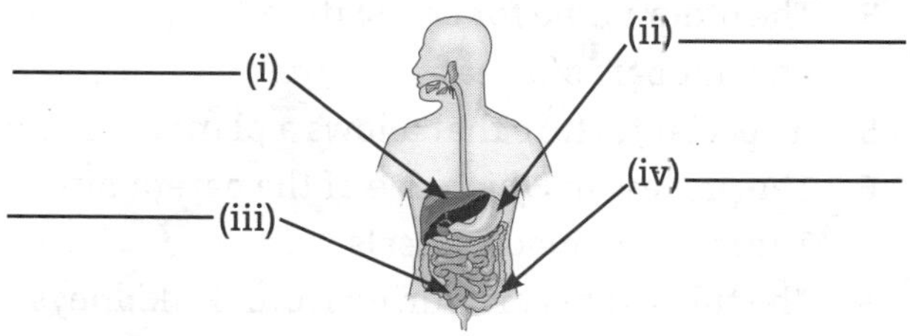

D. Answer the following questions in detail. **(4 × 4 = 16)**

1. Name the main categories of microbes and give one example of each. Can all microbes be called germs? Justify your answer.

2. List two insectivorous plants and explain their adaptations.
3. How are aquatic animals adapted to their habitat?
4. Explain the importance of a balanced diet.

Comprehensive Assessment 2

CHAPTERS 8–14

(Maximum Marks = 50)

A. Name the following. **(10 × 1 = 10)**

1. The process in which germs in water are killed by adding chlorine
2. The breeze that blows during the daytime
3. The soil considered best for the growth of plants
4. The state of matter that takes the shape of the container
5. The liquid that is obtained when a solute dissolves in a solvent
6. The substance that exists in all three states in nature
7. The planet that appears red in the sky
8. The envelope of air around the Earth
9. Another name of man-made fibres
10. The tree-planting festival in India

B. In each of the following questions, two choices are correct. Identify the correct choices. **(9 × 2 = 18)**

1. Which of the following statements are true about the blowing of wind?
   (a) Sun's rays do not fall equally on all parts of the Earth
   (b) Hot air rises upwards
   (c) Earth is round and not flat
   (d) Cool air rises upwards
   (e) Air is made up of different kinds of gases
   (f) Water heats up and cools down faster than land
2. The methods to conserve soil are
   (a) Deforestation (b) Avoid overgrazing (c) Heavy rainfall
   (d) Crop rotation (e) Strong winds (f) Weathering
3. Which of the following are the characteristic features of gases?
   (a) Have fixed shape and volume
   (b) Have fixed volume but no fixed shape
   (c) Can flow in all directions easily
   (d) Less space between the particles
   (e) Can flow only from higher level to lower level
   (f) No fixed shape and volume

4. Which of the following statements are true about solute, solvent and solution?
   (a) The solid that dissolves in liquid is called solvent
   (b) Water is the most important solute
   (c) Salt is an example for solvent
   (d) Solute is uniformly distributed among the particles of solvent
   (e) Solvent dissolves in a solute
   (f) Salt water is an example of solution
5. Which of the following facts are true about the planet 'Venus'?
   (a) Nearest planet to the sun (b) Hottest planet in the solar system
   (c) Brightest planet visible in the sky (d) Smallest planet in the solar system
   (e) Appears as a red planet in the sky (f) Has one moon
6. Which of the following are not forms of energy?
   (a) Light (b) Sound (c) Magnetic (d) Battery (e) Friction (f) Chemical
7. In which of the following cases has work not been done?
   (a) A man pushes a car, the car does not move
   (b) A child kicks a ball into the goalpost
   (c) A bullock pulling a cart down a road
   (d) A cricketer holding a ball
   (e) A lady drawing water from a well
   (f) A man climbing a staircase with a load on his head
8. Which of the following clothes would be suitable for a cold and snowy weather?
   (a) Sweaters (b) Swimsuits (c) Fur jacket
   (d) Cotton shirts (e) T-shirts (f) Shorts
9. We can keep our surroundings green by
   (a) Afforestation (b) Forest fires
   (c) Reducing the use of paper (d) Littering green leaves
   (e) Deforestation (f) Allowing cattle to overgraze

C. Label the diagrams. **(2 × 3 = 6)**

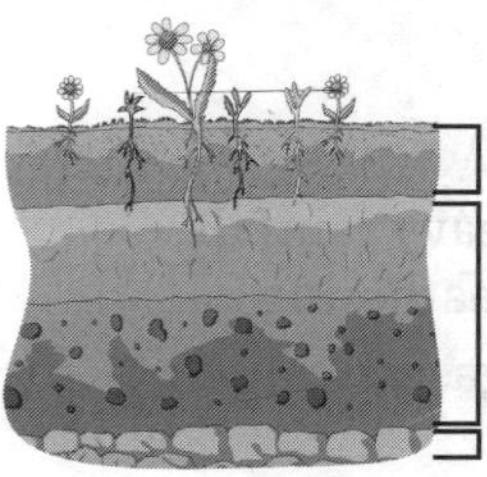

1. ____________
2. ____________
3. ____________

D. Answer the following questions in detail. **(4 × 4 = 16)**

1. Describe soil profile with the help of a diagram.
2. Explain with the help of a diagram how seasons occur on the Earth.
3. Under what conditions do we consider work to be done?
4. Explain the importance of trees.

The Winning Secret

In our village, we wake up by 5.00 am and exercise. Then we have a heavy breakfast and go to school. What do you have for your breakfast, Rahul?
I just have a cup of milk.
That's not enough! We should have a nutritious breakfast, my mother says. What do you have for lunch?
I don't miss my lunch! I am terribly hungry by then.
And what do you do after school, Rahul?
I go home, have some fried snacks and watch TV. That's my favourite part of the day, you know. Then I play computer games for some time, munching some wafers and sipping coke. I finish my homework, study a little, have dinner and go to bed. What do you do after school, Rangan?
I have a glass of milk and go out to play with my friends. We run, cycle and swim in the pond nearby. I return home before it is dark, have a simple meal, finish my homework and then go to bed.
5
5
10

You should also follow good habits like going to bed early, eating healthy food at regular intervals and playing enough outdoor games as part of your exercise.
Thank you, Rangan, for sharing your secret with me. I shall keep these in mind. Bye. See you in the next Sports Meet.
10
I am sure you will be very fit and win the race next time. Bye!

Skills You Need

HANDICRAFTS

Handicrafts are activities that involve making things with your hands in a skillful way. For example, pottery and embroidery.

Handicrafts in India

In ancient India, people lived in colonies called tribals. They used to make handicrafts items for their daily needs. They later started selling these goods in the local markets for other people to use. Nowadays, handicrafts items have become more of decorative items.

India is one of the most culturally rich countries in the world. Indian handicrafts are loved and respected worldwide. India has managed to preserve its artisans and their handicrafts, and many rural artisans earn their livelihood through this means.

Some of the most popular handicrafts of India are woodwork, pottery, jute items, stone carving, shell handicrafts, pashmina shawls, brass handicrafts, bamboo handicrafts, zardozi, phulkaris, silk sarees and carpet weaving.

Pottery

Brass handicrafts

Zardozi work

Shell handicrafts

In India, you can explore many government-approved handicrafts shops such as Dilli Haat in Delhi, Kala Madhyam in Bengaluru and Rajasthali in Jaipur. The handicrafts tradition in India has evolved through generations. The quest for innovation and invention continues to give each craft a contemporary look while preserving the heritage and culture of India.

MAKERSPACE

Let us make a colourful jute-wrapped flower pot!

We need:

A flower pot (clay pot)

Glue gun/glue sticks

Jute rope

Scissors

Acrylic colours

Paint brush

Procedure:

1. Take a flower pot and apply a small stream of glue all around the pot.
2. Start wrapping the jute rope from the bottom and work your way to the top. Make sure to press the jute tightly together so that there are no spaces between each jute layer.
3. Trim off any long strands of loose fibres from the jute to keep the design neat and tidy.
4. Take a paint brush and colour the jute in different colours.

Career Exploration

- Archivists
- Curators and museum workers
- Sculptors
- Fashion designers
- Interior designers
- Graphic designers
- Art directors

Try it!

Make a simple jute rope plant hanger! Or make simple jute rugs!

Happiness Activity Sheets

TEAM SPIRIT!

Team spirit is the feeling of pride and loyalty that exists among the members of a team. This spirit motivates the team to do well or to be the best. It is important not only in sports but also in all parts of school life. It is important when you work on a science project along with your classmates. It is also important when you participate in a quiz competition as a group.

A good team member has the following qualities:

- Recognizes his/her own and everyone's strengths
- Accepts his/her own and other's weaknesses
- Knows when to step up and when to step down
- Collaborates with others and does not escape from doing their share of task
- Says his/her thoughts politely while listening to other's point of view
- Makes decisions together with the other team members
- Takes the win or loss as a team, regardless of his/her own performance

Good team spirit will help you in the following ways:

- You will achieve your team goal quickly.
- You will make more friends.
- You will become more thoughtful and become empathetic, that is understand more about other's feelings and thoughts.
- You will be able to cooperate and encourage each other with honesty.
- You will be able to control your anger if you lose, and support each other instead of blaming others.

Are you aware of your feelings?

Have you ever felt upset or angry while doing a group project (it could be a science project or a sports event)? Write 3–4 words that best describe your feelings in this thought bubble.

How mindful are you?

During a group project, have you ever been not a good team member?

Or are you a great team member?

How do you think you can be a great team member?

Write any five ways in which you are/can become a great team member.

How good is your team spirit!

Collect pictures of a few animals and their habitat. Keep the habitat pictures in a separate box/place. Cut the pictures of animals into six or eight equal squares. Cut the picture in such a way that when the pieces are joined, the entire picture is in place. Arrange your class into 4 groups. Give a picture (the cut pieces) to each group and ask the group to finish the picture by joining all the pieces. Then find the habitat of your animal.

Did your group finish completing the picture first? How did you find the habitat of the animal?

Write down a few words to describe how you felt during this group activity.

Vernacular Names

Butterfly • Assamese: *Pokhila* • Bengali: *Projapoti* • Hindi: *Titalee* • Kannada: *Pataragitti* • Meiteilon: *Kuraak* • Marathi: *Phulapākharū* • Malayalam: *Citraśalabhaṁ* • Mizo: *Phengphehlep* • Tamil: *Pattampuchi* • Telugu: *Sītākōkaciluka* • Urdu: *Titli*

Cactus • Assamese: *kektes* • Hindi: *Kaiktas* • Kannada: *Papus kalli* • Meiteilon: *Tingkhang Lei* • Marathi: *Kĕkṭasa* • Malayalam: *Kaḷḷicceṭi* • Mizo: *Thlalera* • Tamil: *Kaṟṟāḻai* • Telugu: *Kākṭas* • Urdu: *Kekts*

Duckweed • Assamese: *Barpuni, jalakumbhi* • Bengali: *Pana* • Hindi: *Jalakumbhi* • Kannada: *Antaragange, kumbik* • Meiteilon: *Kang* • Marathi: *Akashamuli, jalamandavi, paankumbhi* • Malayalam: *Akasathamara, kodappayal, mutta payal, neercheera* • Tamil: *Akasha-t-tamarai, antara-t-tamarai, kuli-t-tamarai* • Telugu: *Antara-tamara, budaga tamara, akashatamara, neeraaku, nirubudiki, tudikura* • Urdu: *Khazah*

Hawk • Assamese: *Sanacholey* • Bengali: *Bajpakhi* • Hindi: *Baaz* • Kannada: *Giduga* • Malayalam: *Parunt* • Meiteilon: *Uchithembi* • Marathi: *Bahiri sasana* • Mizo: *Mu* • Tamil: *Parunt* • Telugu: *Hak* • Urdu: *Hok*

Hydrilla • Assamese: *Pani-birina* • Bengali: *Jhanjhi, kureli* • Hindi: *Jhangi, kureli* • Kannada: *Haiḍrillā* • Meiteilon: *Charang* • Marathi: *Seval, Shakharisheval* • Malayalam: *Ene-pael* • Tamil: *Amiranappaci, cikavalakam, cimpaka* • Telugu: *Poonaachu, valakada* • Urdu: *hīḍdrila*

Moss • Assamese: *Mas* • Bengali: *Shaaola* • Hindi: *Kaee* • Kannada: *Paachi* • Meiteilon: *Isang* • Marathi: *Mŏsa* • Malayalam: *Mēās* • Mizo: *Lung sam* • Tamil: *Pāci* • Telugu: *Nācu* • Urdu: *Kai*

Pitcher plant • Assamese: *Kolochi-goch* • Bengali: *kalash udbhid, ghotopotri* • Hindi: *Mataka sanyantr* • Kannada: *Picar sasya, Katu senai, Amu-mani-gidda* • Marathi: *Picara vanaspatī* • Malayalam: *Piccar plānṟ* • Tamil: *Kuṭam ālai* • Telugu: *Maṭṭi mokka* • Urdu: *khadaka phuta*

Polar bear • Assamese: *Tusara beluka* • Hindi: *Dhruveey bhaaloo* • Kannada: *Hima karadi* • Meiteilon: *Sa-om* • Marathi: *Dhruvīya asvala* • Malayalam: *Dhruvakkaraṭi* • Tamil: *Turuva karaṭi* • Telugu: *Dhruva elugubaṇṭi* • Urdu: *Qatbi Reech*

Squirrel• Assamese: *Kerketuwa* • Bengali: *Kathberali* • Hindi: Gilaharee • Kannada: *Alilu* • Malayalam: *Annan* • Meiteilon: *Kheiroi* • Marathi: *Gilaharee* • Mizo: *Thehlei* • Tamil: *Anil* • Telugu: *Udata* • Urdu: *Gilaharee*

Whale • Assamese: *Timi* • Bengali: *Timi* • Hindi: *Vhel* • Kannada: *Timingala* • Meiteilon: *Vhel* • Marathi: *Dēvamāsā* • Malayalam: *Timiṅgalaṁ* • Mizo: *Nghapui* • Tamil: *Timiṅkilam* • Telugu: *Timiṅgalaṁ* • Urdu: *Minke*

Yak • Assamese: *Yak* • Bengali: *Chamri gai* • Hindi: *Yaak* • Kannada: *Chamarimruga* • Meiteilon: *Yak* • Marathi: *Yāka* • Malayalam: *Malankaala* • Tamil: *Kavariman* • Telugu: *Yāk* • Urdu: *Yak*

What do you call these plants and animals in your language? Share the names with us at **schoolsupport@harpercollins.co.in**